DECISION
◂ POINT ▸

DECISION POINT

The Business Game That Lets You Make the Decision and Reap the Rewards... Or Bear the Consequences

Robert B. Nelson

TEN SPEED PRESS
Berkeley, California

ACKNOWLEDGEMENTS

The following people played an integral role in shaping and reviewing portions of this book. Their involvement made the cases more realistic, and the development of the book more enjoyable! Many thanks to: Peter Economy, Dan Fetler, Matt Kantor, Mike McManus, Doug Nelson, Greg Sasaki, Sam Steinhardt, Austin Speed, Bill Taylor, Jennifer Wallick, and John Weiskoff.

Ten Speed Press
P.O. Box 7123
Berkeley, California 94707

First Ten Speed Press Printing 1992

Cover design by Fifth Street Design
Text design by Sarah Levin
Typesetting by Ann Flanagan Typography

Library of Congress Cataloging-in-Publication Data

Nelson, Robert B.
Decision point / Robert B. Nelson.
p. cm.
ISBN 0-89815-485-5 :
1. Decision-making—Case studies. I. Title.
HD30.23.N44 1992
858.4'03—dc20 92-23759
CIP

Printed in the United States of America

1 2 3 4 5 — 96 95 94 93 92

Contents

FOREWORD

It's refreshing to read a book that makes learning fun. *Decision Point* is such a book. It grabs you and pulls you into different worlds of business where priorities, values, and objectives differ but where the ways people are managed and effective decisions are made often remain the same. Although entertaining and fun, *Decision Point* is based upon well-researched and validated theories of decision making and management. The theories are built into the book in a way that doesn't distract or burden the reader, yet allows you to sense the trade-offs and consequences of different approaches to handling the various problems presented.

Bob has done a wonderful job of developing an interactive format for the book that provides immediate, ongoing feedback about decisions as they are made. You gain insight into how to be more effective in handling people and situations in the cases that are presented; implicitly, you learn real-life business skills that can be transferred to your own business environment. As a side benefit, you get a fascinating view of the inner workings of three very different industries: the film industry, management consulting, and robotics manufacturing. This "slice of life" approach presents an exciting and accurate picture of the daily challenges key executives encounter in those businesses. You'll learn about factors that are necessary for success, decisions that are deemed crucial, and variables that influence decision makers in each industry.

I especially like the fact that *Decision Point* reflects reality. Several examples come to mind:

1. *There are no "right" or "wrong" answers.* In much the same way, our choices in managing real-life people and situations are relative, as well. What works with one person in one situation may be entirely inappropriate on another occasion.

2. *In some situations, the best action to take is to do nothing at all.* This is an important lesson! Managers often feel compelled to expend great amounts of time and energy trying to solve a problem that is apt to go away if ignored.

3. *In some situations, the rationally "best" choice of alternatives still fails.* Even with ample information and a good business sense, unknown factors sometimes make a shambles of the best-laid plans. You must learn to cope with chance, bad luck, and random variables in *Decision Point* much as one encounters in life.

I enjoyed the analysis at the end of each case, which gives insight about what you did (or could have done) to be successful. The Appendix also provides valuable information about your decision-making style as based upon your cumulative responses in all three cases. With all of this feedback, every reader is apt to pick up quite a few tips on how to be more effective in dealing with people and problems in his or her own job.

In the final analysis, it's not so important how successful you are in these cases (although it is fun to accumulate points and see the direct impact of your decisions). What is important is the way this book causes you to refect about how you approach people, problems, and decisions in real life. It allows you to consider other approaches that you normally might not consider and to see the positive consequences that may come from trying new behaviors. If you gain just a single technique or idea which you can use to be more effective in your own working environment, you should definitely feel you got your money's worth. If you have the fun I did in the process—all the better!

Kenneth H. Blanchard,
author of *The One Minute Manager*

INTRODUCTION

You are about to embark on a journey into the working lives of three senior executives in three very different industries. You'll encounter decisions they have to make on a daily basis and you'll be given an opportunity to test your skill in making similar decisions, with a chance to see the consequences of your selections. Some decisions will be minor and routine, others will be crucial to the overall success of your firm. All decisions will have some impact on the final outcome of your efforts. You have to decide which action is appropriate at each decision point from the alternatives presented, and which decisions are key to the overall success of your objectives.

Based upon each selection you make, you will be given positive, negative, or zero points and some feedback concerning your decision. Keep track of the number/letter designations of your choices and the total points you have accumulated as you progress through each of the three cases. Total points earned and specific decision choices you made will be used to determine your overall success on each case. Your decision selections will also be used to give you feedback on the style and consistency of your decision-making ability.

Your overall success will be a function of your skill in decision making, and your management and general business sense. Luck or unforeseen circumstances will, at times, be a variable, either helping or hindering your progress in an unpredictable way.

These cases have been designed to be realistic. The author conducted numerous personal interviews and did extensive research into the various industries presented. Each case has, in addition, been reviewed by managers and professionals who work in these industries, and many of their comments have been integrated into the supporting discussions.

CASE #1

Amalgamated Films, Unlimited

BRIEFING

You are a Hollywood producer about to embark upon the packaging, production, and release of your most recent film. Until recently, you were an independent film producer whose firm put together deals and then attempted to place the projects with major studios. One of the seven major studios subsequently underwrote the costs of production and promotion of the films, usually over $20 million.

Your film company, Amalgamated Films, Unlimited, has recently been acquired by a multi-national corporation, Conglomerate Enterprises. The parent company will pick up the costs of films you will produce (giving you greater security), but will have a say in approving your expenditures (giving you less control).

Although you are an experienced producer with a solid reputation, you can easily produce a bomb if you are not careful with the daily decisions you have to make. Seemingly minor decisions can explode into major problems, and important decisions can slip by without the level of consideration and action that they deserve. You need to use good sense and sound business judgement to identify the most important decisions and respond to them appropriately.

In the upcoming pages, you will be able to test your business savvy with seven basic decisions and multiple subdecisions related to the production and promotion of the film. Write down the letters of the decisions as you make them (1D, 2A, and so on) and keep track of the total number of points that you accrue to evaluate your overall success at the end of the case and to obtain an analysis of your decision-making style at the end of the book. Good luck!

Industry Description

The film industry is a very risky and unpredictable business. Less than three of every ten films produced earn a profit and an additional one out of ten films breaks even. The rest lose money for various reasons, sometimes reasons that experts in the industry cannot predict or even accurately identify after the fact. It is always difficult to guess what public taste will be in two years—the amount of time it usually takes a film to reach the market from its conception.

The average studio film costs $17 to 25 million to produce with at least $5 to 9 million usually being spent on a P & A (prints and ads) campaign after it is released. With so much money at risk, studios often are loathe to take risks, and seek to bet on what seem to be sure winners—namely, spin-offs of current hits. This strategy often works, although it tends to produce formulaic movies which at times involve few creative innovations. In addition, as a successful formula becomes identified, several of the major studios rush to produce similar films and a competitive glut emerges. The strategy fails when a popular movie trend suddenly shifts, often in unpredictable and unexplained ways.

Studios try to minimize losses in a variety of ways in the likelihood that the film is not as successful as anticipated. Star talent (actors/actresses and directors) associated with a film can help line up distribution and can pull a strong audience response. Excellent special effects can do the same. Increasingly, success in the film industry is becoming dependent upon multi-markets such as special deals regarding subsidiary rights over home video, overseas distribution, cable, books, toys, music, and so on can help to cover expenses of a film and produce additional revenue streams. Heavy promotion can often make a fair film turn a profit and/or a good film into a blockbuster. Of course, a good story helps, but many films (sad to say) have become financially successful with a poor or minimal plot, and even more so if the plot is simple enough to easily spawn one or more sequels.

Film companies are being increasingly run by professional managers—

MBAs—who are often accused of not having a good feel for what it takes to make a successful movie (and Conglomerate Enterprises is no exception). MBAs are trained in quantitative skills that translate poorly to an industry which is founded on creative ideas and strong intuitive beliefs. Those in management who don't achieve success—or who are responsible for an expensive film that fails badly—are replaced, usually every few years. Careers, like the companies in which they exist, are unstable. Individuals in the industry are often anxious or even at times, paranoid. Egos run rampant.

Films are increasingly packaged and produced by independent contractors on a project-by-project basis. Pulling together a wide range of talent to work on a project for a short, intense period of time adds to the unpredictable nature of the final product. Often promotion strategies have to be shifted when a completed film turns out quite different from the original concept after millions of dollars have already been invested. Good stories are, at times, a secondary consideration to the timely packaging of an attractive deal which seems likely to make money—if only on paper.

Firm Description

Amalgamated Films was an independent film company which has recently become a subsidiary of a large multi-national corporation, Conglomerate Enterprises. There exists a strong clash of personalities, philosophies, motivations, and organizational cultures between the business-oriented corporate management and the creatively oriented film personnel. Personnel at Amalgamated are used to autonomy and resist and resent interference from above. Directors believe their vision is the most important to the artistic, and consequently the commercial, success of the films they produce.

Reader Role

You are a film producer for Amalgamated Films, a position that is perhaps the least defined of any position in the film industry. The producer is with the film the longest of anyone, and usually has the overall responsibility for the film's success. A good producer has to have many skills which include: the ability to visualize a film from a script and understand its value and potential; the ability to be a good business negotiator, fund raiser, recruiter, and so on; and the ability to be diplomatic in arbitrating and resolving disputes as they arise. Many producers also have screenwriting and acting experience as well. In fact, the trend of successful producers today is to "hyphenate," that is, have a broad base of skills to draw from (thus be a writer-producer-director).

Your objective is to produce successful movies—hopefully, blockbuster films—but since the odds of such success are small, you will be pleased to make a film that is a solid success (pays back approximately three times its cost—the amount necessary to begin earning a profit). Besides aiming for a significant "upside potential" (the best that can happen), you will want to do all you can to protect your "downside risk" (the worst that can happen), in case the film is not extremely successful. In some instances, ancillary deals can be arranged prior to the production of a film to assure a minimum financial return on the project. At the very least, you will want to cover your sunk costs (funds actually spent), although this may not—as in real life—always be possible.

In this case, the producer (you) reports to corporate management, and the film's director (who you hired) reports to you. The producer must mediate between the formal policies and procedures of corporate management and the demanding and, at times, eccentric and irrational style of the film's director.

The Decisions

Decision #1: Budget Allocation

"This is a great script!" you say out loud, "I haven't seen material this fresh in years!" Your mind immediately starts to whirl as you mentally piece together elements of a deal that can make this film, *Kingdom Come,* a success. Your firm, Amalgamated Films, already owns the property—it was part of a five-package option you acquired based on prototypes. It fits the budget you have in mind ($16 to 22 million). You liked the treatment, but now, after reviewing the entire script (one of over 10,000 your company received this year), you really believe it has the potential to break out. The market seems headed toward action-drama films that are more sophisticated in plot and characterization (so says your marketing department, at least), and you think you can capitalize on the trend. You already have a tentative commitment from George Ruckus to direct the picture. He had read an earlier treatment and loved the concept. The leading part seems a natural for Robert Renford, and you immediately call his agent and describe the project:

YOU: ...so it's got all the elements for Box Office Gold—is Renford available?

AGENT: He's just wrapping up a shoot, and has locked-in bookings for the next six months. His schedule opens up a bit then, and he might be available. Sounds like the type of story he'd consider, but I've got to tell you, his rates have gone up. We're looking for $7 million up front and a percentage of the gross.

YOU: That's a steep ticket... what size percentage?

AGENT: Ten points.

YOU: I'll send you the script for Renford to review. Meanwhile, let me think about those terms.

You hang up the phone and think about the consequences of having Renford as part of the deal. It could be a big plus—if he's available and willing to do it. Having him associated with the film will make it easier to sell the project to Corporate and more likely to predict a sizable minimum draw when the film hits the streets. At the same time, the film will be more expensive with Renford on board and thus there will be a higher breakeven point (the point at which your sunk costs are recouped), which will make it more difficult to make money on the deal. Since 50 percent of the gross already goes to distributors and 50 percent of the remaining proceeds go to the investors who put up the funding, and another $500,000 or so is needed to pay interest, the film will need to make 2½ to 3 times its cost to be profitable.

The overall production and promotion budget you put together will be in excess of $15 million. Seven million dollars is a lot of money, yet recognized talent is a good place to invest it. Getting the ten points might be worth taking a lower advance to Renford, depending upon how well he thinks the picture could do. If you can hook him on the concept, perhaps he'll be willing to negotiate. Who knows, maybe he doesn't have anything lined up and his terms will be flexible. Or maybe you can cut down his role so it will be less work for him. You don't, however, want to insult him by haggling over a few million.

Haggling over a few million? Are you crazy? What about all the lesser known, up-and-coming talent that would work well in the leading role at a fraction of this price—without any percentage?!

Then again, no one is forcing you to spend the lion's share of the budget on one actor. Depending upon how you slant the screenplay you could put extra money into some impressive special effects (additional action shots, special set construction, electronics, and so on) which would especially make sense if you wanted to emphasis the action scenes in the film. Special effects have made many films extremely successful that had largely unknown talent when released: Witness the success of *Jaws, Star Wars, Raiders of the Lost Ark,* and numerous others.

Alternatively, you could invest in an original musical score for the film. The importance of a quality soundtrack cannot be understated. Besides the additional sales of CDs and cassettes, the music (if it becomes popular) becomes built-in advertising when it receives airtime on radio stations. The hit movie *American Graffiti,* which only had a budget of $750,000, had $90,000 of it allocated to music—an enormous percentage and a large number of hit songs for a single film! *Chariots of Fire* had a terrible script, and no name actors, but an excellent commercial score which contributed immensely to the film's financial success. Those bets paid off and yours could too!

Of course, you could put additional money into script development. Good dialogue, pace, and suspense are all important elements of many successful films. The extra attention might increase your chances of an Academy Award—an honor that usually brings at least a $10 million additional return in the market.

You think through the possible alternatives, then select your priority for allocation of your budget.

YOUR CHOICE

1A Go after the name talent. See below.

1B Emphasize special effects. See page 10.

1C Invest in a quality musical soundtrack. See page 10.

1D Give added attention to script development. See page 11.

1E None of the above at this time. See page 11.

1A **Go after the name talent.**

Great! A big name is like a trademark that can draw the viewing public.

+1 Point; Please Continue . . .

What do you want to offer Renford?

YOUR CHOICE

1F Offer Renford $7 million with no percent. See page 12.

1G Offer Renford $7 million and 3 percent. See page 12.

1H Accept Renford's agent's initial terms. See page 13.

1B **Emphasize special effects.**

Special effects are hot! To be effective, they have to be really impressive (and, if possible, novel) to attract an ever-sophisticated viewing audience in this high-tech age. You will probably want to slant the story/script accordingly to emphasize the action elements of the film.

+1 Point; Please Continue...

Even if the film will be more action oriented, you can still invest in a name for the film. Chuck Morris might do nicely, and Michael Sheen is still quite affordable. Or do you want to put the available funds elsewhere?

YOUR CHOICE

1I Go after other name talent. See page 13.

1J Invest in a quality musical soundtrack. See page 14.

1K Give added attention to script development. See page 14.

1L Allocate additional funds to marketing and promotion. See page 15.

1M Undecided at present where to allocate additional funds. See page 15.

1C **Invest in a quality musical soundtrack.**

Sounds good! Good music can help the film in many ways, as already discussed.

+1 Point; Please Continue...

The investment in music is substantially less than having big name talent, leaving you financial resources that can still be allocated. What is your preference for these resources?

YOUR CHOICE

1I Go after other name talent. See page 13.

1K Give added attention to script development. See page 14.

1N Allocate additional funds for special effects. See page 15.

1O Allocate additional funds to marketing and promotion. See page 16.

1M Undecided at present where to allocate funds. See page 15.

1D **Give added attention to script development.**

This is a good choice, since a strong script can greatly improve a film's appeal.

+3 Points; Choose Again:

The story will probably cost you $100,000 initially, and your script development might run another $250,000. You still have some room in the budget—where would you like to allocate funds?

YOUR CHOICE

1I Go after other name talent. See page 13.

1J Invest in a quality musical soundtrack. See page 14.

1N Allocate additional funds for special effects. See page 15.

1O Allocate additional funds to marketing and promotion. See page 16.

1M Undecided at present where to allocate additional funds. See page 15.

1E **None of the above.**

Are you kidding?! This film has to have something going for it!

−4 Points; Choose Again:

1A Go after other name talent. See page 13.

1B Emphasize special effects. See page 10.

1C Invest in a quality musical soundtrack. See page 10.

1D Give added attention to script development. See page 11.

1F Offer Renford $7 million and no percent.

Your offer is rejected. Renford's agent is holding firm to his initial demands.

0 Points; Choose Again:

YOUR CHOICE

1G Offer Renford $7 million and 3 percent. See below.

1H Accept the agent's initial terms. See page 13.

1P Counteroffer Renford $4 million and 7 percent. See page 16.

1Q Select a lesser talent for a more manageable price. See page 16.

1G Offer Renford $7 million and 3 percent.

Your offer is rejected. Renford's agent counteroffers $7 million and 7 percent.

0 Points; Choose Again:

YOUR CHOICE

1Q Select a lesser talent for a more manageable price. See page 16.

1R Accept the agent's counteroffer. See page 17.

1S Offer Renford $7 million and 5 percent. See page 18.

1H **Accept the agent's initial terms.**

Congratulations, you have just signed some "bankable talent." Although the price is expensive, in this business it is money well spent because many other key elements pertaining to this film (financing, promotion, and so on) will now be much easier. You might have gotten him cheaper had you negotiated, but his rates are well known. The chances of success of the film, although never guaranteed, are now much stronger with the name talent.

+3 Points; Please Continue...

Renford's agent calls back and says Renford has received another offer and now needs an additional $500,000 to commit to your deal. What do you do?

YOUR CHOICE

1T Hold firm to the initial agreement. See page 18.

1U Reluctantly agree to the additional money. See page 19.

1I **Go after other name talent.**

You are able to line up some less expensive, yet well known talent, which leaves you more room in the budget to increase other items, if you'd like.

+3 Points; Please Continue...

What is your next priority for allocating available funds?

YOUR CHOICE

1J Invest in a quality musical soundtrack. See page 14.

1L Allocate additional funds to marketing and promotion. See page 15.

1N Allocate additional funds for special effects. See page 15.

1V Allocate additional funds to script development. See page 19.

1M Undecided at present where to allocate additional funds. See page 15.

1J **Invest in a quality musical soundtrack.**

Good music will always be a plus for the film!

+1 Point; Please Continue...

Is there another preference you have for allocating available funds in the budget?

YOUR CHOICE

(Do not select a choice previously made.)

1L Allocate additional funds to marketing and promotion. See page 15.

1N Allocate additional funds for special effects. See page 15.

1M Undecided at present where to allocate additional funds. See page 15.

1K **Give added attention to script development.**

Without high-quality acting, a high quality script is wasted.

−2 Points; Please Continue...

If you have not lined up your primary acting talent, go to Decision 1Q, page 16; otherwise, go to Decision #2, page 21.

1L **Allocate additional funds to marketing and promotions.**

Based upon your expressed priorities for this film, additional funding for marketing and promotions should be a good investment.

+2 Points, Please Continue...

If you have not lined up your primary acting talent, go to Decision 1Q, page 16; otherwise, go to Decision #2, page 21.

1M **Undecided at present where to allocate additional funds.**

Guess what? Corporate just decided for you! They decided that you don't need the money and will be retaining the unallocated portion of the budget in the corporate coffers until further notice.

−1 Point; Go to Decision #2, page 21.

1N **Allocate additional funds for special effects.**

Corporate likes your suggestion! They feel it would be wise to enhance the action-adventure angle of the film, and the funds are placed in the budget for special effects. Of course, you will have to slant the story and script accordingly...

+2 Points; Choose Again:

(Select only choices not previously made.)

1J Invest in a quality musical soundtrack. See page 14.

1J Allocate additional funds to marketing and promotion. See page 15.

1V Allocate additional funds to script development. See page 19.

1M Undecided at present where to allocate additional funds. See page 15.

1O Allocate additional funds for marketing and promotion.

Without name talent, Corporate doesn't feel additional promotion would be effective. They deny your request and retain the funds.

−2 Points; Go to Decision #2, page 21.

1P Counteroffer Renford $4 million and 7 percent.

Your offer is rejected! Renford's agent counteroffers at $6 million and 10 percent.

0 Points; Choose Again:

1Q Select a lesser talent for a more reasonable price. See below.

1R Accept the agent's counteroffer. See page 17.

1S Offer Renford $6 million and 5 percent. See page 18.

1Q Select a lesser talent for a more manageable price.

You may have just saved Conglomerate Enterprises lots of money, but you also significantly lowered the odds of the film making money. Without recognized talent it's going to be more difficult for you to obtain adequate financing, draw a name director, and market the film—no matter how good the story is! Don't despair, however, you may still beat the odds or perhaps produce a sleeper. Many films, of course, have been extremely successful without name talent, especially those in the action-adventure or sci-fi genres. *Back to the Future,* is just one such successful example (and it had been turned down by nine studios!).

−5 Points; Please Continue . . .

You saved $3 million dollars on the projected budget for the film. You can slant the script more towards action-adventure and allocate additional funds for special effects or you could put more money into development of a memorable musical score; or you could spend it on additional marketing and promotion. How would you like to allocate additional funds?

YOUR CHOICE

1J Invest in a quality musical soundtrack. See page 14.

1K Give added attention to script development. See page 14.

1N Allocate additional funds for special effects. See page 15.

1O Allocate additional funds to marketing and promotion. See page 16.

1M Undecided at present how to allocate additional funds. See page 15.

1R **Accept the agent's counteroffer.**

Wise choice—Renford was about to lose interest in the project. Using him in the leading role will cost you some money but the potential for the film's financial success is now much better. Plus you successfully negotiated better terms for the contract.

+7 Points; Please Continue...

What is your second priority for allocating funds in your budget?

YOUR CHOICE

1J Invest in a quality musical soundtrack. See page 14.

1L Allocate additional funds to marketing and promotion. See page 15.

1V Allocate additional funds to script development. See page 19.

1W Emphasize funds to special effects. See page 19.

1M Undecided at present where to allocate additional funds. See page 15.

1S **Offer Renford $7 million and 5 percent.**

Your offer is rejected! Renford's agent says he is no longer interested in the project. Your deliberations seem to have cost you a lost opportunity. You could find an excuse to come back with a higher offer ("Corporate authorized increased funding"), or just forget it.

0 Points; Choose Again:

1X Quickly call the agent back with an increased offer. See page 20.

1Y Wait until next week, then call the agent back with an increased offer. See page 20.

1Z Forget Renford and his agent. See page 20.

1T **Hold firm to the initial agreement.**

You might have thought that Renford's agent was just trying to get a better deal, but apparently he was telling the truth. Renford declines your script. Fortunately for you, your second choice for the role, Raoul Numan, is interested in the film and agrees to substantially more affordable terms.

+2 Points; Please Continue...

What is your second priority for your budget?

YOUR CHOICE

1J Invest in a quality musical soundtrack. See page 14.

1L Allocate additional funds to marketing and promotion. See page 15.

1V Allocate additional funds to script development. See page 19.

1N Allocate additional funds for special effects. See page 15.

1M Undecided at present where to allocate additional funds. See page 15.

1U **Reluctantly agree to the additional money.**

This is not the way to negotiate! You had a deal, and if necessary, you should walk away from it to protect your integrity. You got Renford, but it cost you much more than it should have.

−3 Points, Go to Decision #2, page 43.

1V **Allocate additional funds to script development.**

Given you now have a talented actor involved with the project, an improved script should capitalize on his ability as well as his name.

+2 Points; Choose Again:

(Do not select a choice previously made.)

1J Invest in a quality musical soundtrack. See page 14.

1L Allocate additional funds to marketing and promotion. See page 15.

1N Allocate additional funds for special effects. See page 15.

1M Undecided at present where to allocate additional funds. See page 15.

1W **Emphasize special effects.**

Corporate thinks an increased special effects budget is unnecessary with a draw like Renford and thus denies the increase in funds.

−1 Point; Choose Again:

1J Invest in a quality musical soundtrack. See page 14.

1L Allocate additional funds to marketing and promotion. See page 16.

1V Give added attention to script development. See above.

1M Undecided at present where to allocate additional funds. See page 15.

1X **Quickly call Renford's agent back with an increased offer.**

Your offer is accepted! You got Renford, although it cost you more than you expected it would.

+2 Points; Please Continue...

What is your second priority for your budget?

YOUR CHOICE

1J Invest in a quality musical soundtrack. See page 14.

1L Allocate additional funds to marketing and promotion. See page 16.

1V Allocate additional funds to script development. See page 19.

1W Emphasize special effects. See page 19.

1M Undecided at present where to allocate additional funds. See page 15.

1Y **Wait until next week, then call the agent back with an increased offer.**

You certainly don't have much sense of timing, do you? Renford's agent laughs and hangs up on you...

−3 Points; Default to Decision 1Q, page 16.

1Z **Forget Renford and his agent.**

It obviously was not meant to be.

0 Points; Default to Decision 1Q, page 16.

DECISION #2: DIRECTOR PERKS

"You don't understand!" you state, trying to control your temper, "Corporate policy is very clear on these matters. There is no way you can have a Mercedes-Benz for a company car! To begin with, Conglomerate Enterprises has a leasing agreement with Ford for LTD's and we can't legally make exceptions. In addition, even if I could get it approved by Corporate—which I doubt—there are dozens of higher-ranking and more qualified executives in this corporation who will be upset because they can't have a company car of their choice as well. This subsidiary doesn't need that type of bad press throughout the Corporation."

You were quite pleased to have lined up George Ruckus to direct your film. Corporate also seemed satisfied: They not only agreed to do the film, they also left the budget you proposed intact. You had, however, forgotten about Ruckus' reputation for being temperamental. Your memory is now being jogged...

"Well, think it over. I see the position it puts you in with regard to other executives and the like, but quite frankly, I could care less," Ruckus says flatly. He is his usual blunt self, almost beaming with blatant disrespect for authority. "I'm taking quite a risk with my reputation by directing this film. It's hardly the same as a secure desk job. I expect to be treated in a manner indicative of my status in the film industry, not merely in the limited confines of this organization. If they want to skimp, tell them to cut back on their administrative overhead, of which they are likely a redundant part! Just don't mess with me or my film."

Ruckus storms out of the office, slamming the door behind him. The entire incident strikes you as a bit unprofessional on his part. You don't quite see how Ruckus could get so upset about not having a Mercedes while shooting this film. It's almost as though he sees the issue symbolically as an attempt to limit his influence. It's clear that he is not going to settle for a "no," simply because some policy manual lying on a desk in a glass building in the middle of L.A. says so. He won't be stifled by a bureaucratic system for which he has no respect.

This is hardly the way you want to begin your relationship with your new director. Whatever the reasons, the issue is apparently important to

Ruckus. And if it is important to Ruckus, it is important you, because Ruckus is a crucial element for the success of *Kingdom Come*. He has the track record that this film needs. You were lucky to get him to agree to direct it, and you want him to be happy and motivated enough to do a good job. Your relationship is just beginning and you want him to know you are on his side—that the film is a team effort.

Still, is capitulating on this issue a good precedent to set in your relationship with Ruckus? Would you have to continue to give in on numerous other issues to keep him happy? Shouldn't you be strict about matters pertaining to the budget? Will your superiors at the corporate office understand the situation, or are they more likely to consider you an ineffective manager who feels compelled to bring even petty problems to their attention?

In short, is it worth the aggravation to make a stand in support of Ruckus on this issue, or will you be wasting what precious little clout you have with Corporate—and damage your reputation in the process? After considering the pros and cons of these considerations, you arrange a meeting to speak with Ruckus to tell him what you have decided.

YOUR CHOICE

2A Deny the deviation from corporate policy. See below.

2B Tell Ruckus you'll see what you can do. See page 23.

2C Tell Ruckus he can have the Mercedes if he pays the difference in the lease costs. See page 24.

2D Agree to fight for the deviation from corporate policy. See page 24.

2A Deny the deviation from corporate policy.

Ruckus might have been upset before, but now he is hopping mad! He starts waving his arms and yelling and generally creating quite an unpleasant scene. He gives you a long sermon about bureaucratic incompetence and lack of support and his own value that concludes with an ultimatum: Get approval for the Mercedes or find a new director.

You think he may be bluffing, using his flair for drama, but you can't be sure. You reconsider how important it really is to have him on the project. After all, who's in control anyway?

At any rate, you have definitely damaged your working relationship, hopefully, not beyond repair.

−1 Point; Choose Again:

(Do not select a choice previously made.)

YOUR CHOICE

2B Tell Ruckus you'll see what you can do. See page 23.

2C Tell Ruckus he can have the Mercedes if he pays the difference in the lease costs. See page 24.

2D Agree to fight for the deviation from corporate policy. See page 24.

2E Stand firm in your decision to deny the deviation. See page 25.

2F Attempt to sign a new director as a back-up. See page 25.

2B Tell Ruckus that you'll see what you can do.

Surprisingly little, as expected. Your superior at Corporate expresses her concern about the negative attention it would bring to the business unit and the criticism she'd have to put up with on a daily basis from other executives. She discusses the need to keep a lid on expenses so they don't escalate unnecessarily. Still, she concludes with leaving it up to you. She says she would support you no matter what your final decision is. You reconsider the consequences and return to discuss the issue with Ruckus.

0 Points; Choose Again:

YOUR CHOICE

2A Deny the deviation from corporate policy. See page 22.

2C Tell Ruckus he can have the Mercedes if he pays the difference in the lease costs. See page 24.

2D Agree to fight for the deviation from corporate policy. See page 24.

2C **Tell Ruckus he can have the Mercedes if he pays the difference in lease costs.**

Ruckus refuses and is insulted by your offer. He names three other directors who drive Mercedes—each of whom, he claims, is his inferior in reputation and talent.

+1 Point; Choose Again:

YOUR CHOICE

2A Deny the deviation from corporate policy. See page 22.

2D Agree to fight for the deviation from corporate policy. See page 24.

2F Attempt to sign a new director as a back-up. See page 25.

2D **Agree to fight for the deviation from corporate policy.**

You may have lost points with the folks at Corporate, but you just made a friend of your new director. Hopefully, Ruckus won't take advantage of you and continue to press for special favors and perks. Your superior will take some flack as well and, as she advised, it may indeed be a poor precedent for future project expenses. But the project is launched on a happy note, a team spirit prevails, and Ruckus is already telling people how you stood up to the corporation for him.

+3 Points; Please Continue...

Unfortunately, another executive complains and you receive an edict from Corporate to disallow the exception you had granted regarding Ruckus' company car. What would you like to do about this?

YOUR CHOICE

2G Comply with the edict. See page 26.

2H Ignore the edict. See page 26.

2E **Stand firm in your decision to deny the deviation.**

Ruckus quits!

Select from the following two choices, as appropriate:

#1 **If you have a back-up director signed on...**

+3 Points; Go to Decision #3, page 26.

OR

2F **Attempt to sign up a new director as a back-up.**

Good news! Steve Steelburg is interested in the project! He will cost you a little more, but agrees not to request a Mercedes.

+1 Point; Choose Again:

YOUR CHOICE

2A Deny the deviation. See page 22.

2G Tell Ruckus his contract is cancelled. See below.

2G **Tell Ruckus his contract is cancelled.**

Ruckus says that's not necessary—he quits! You see it as a blessing in disguise, although it sets the schedule back one month as the new director gets organized.

+1 Point; Go to Decision #3, page 26.

2H Ignore the edict.

Ignoring this communication from Corporate will save you much frustration. If confronted on this fact, you can claim total ignorance of the matter—you never received the memo. After all, if the film is successful, the issue will be forgotten. In addition, be sure to avoid the executive who had the strongest objections....

+2 Points; Go to Decision #3, below.

Decision #3: Ethics and Artistic Merit

The "dailies" are always an enjoyable part of a film shoot. Getting to see the day's work in review and trying to guess which takes will make it past the editing process to the final film is fun. You're almost halfway through the shooting, and everything seems to be going well. You've stopped in on occasion to watch some of the clips and you have been quite pleased with the quality of the material. Something in this particular scene, however, bothers you. You listen to the dialogue taking place on the screen:

"Well, you couldn't do it in our country, that's for sure. We might be the home of the brave and the defender of the faiths, but when it comes to free trade, freedom stops at the border. Let those foreigners pay a premium for the privilege of doing business in the U.S., but if you dare try to squeeze the profit margin of American business, you'll surely reap the wrath of these people."

It seems that the film has taken on a bias against big business. At times it is an undertone or sarcasm, but often it is more blatant. In this scene, for example, it is almost a sermon...

"Don't give me that anti-trust crap! The railroads made this country what it is, and the oil companies will keep it there. If they say our country needs nuclear power, that's good enough for me."

"That's your problem, Jake. You've got so much blind trust in the American way, you can't recognize when it's robbing you blind. The oil companies aren't into nuclear power and alternative energy sources because it's good for our country, they're there to protect—and guarantee—their future profits. They know that simply merging with other oil industrials is too obvious a move for the Justice Department to allow, but they can get away with investing in seemingly unrelated industries—and increase their stranglehold on the consumer in the process!"

You were aware the director had made some script changes, but you didn't realize they were quite this extreme. This type of shift is more common than you'd like to admit in the industry as films take on personalities of their own—often in different and unpredictable ways that differ greatly from the original screenplay. Somehow you don't think these new changes will go over too big when the board of directors of your parent company screens the film. Their negative reaction could easily place a crimp on the level of support the film will get once it is released.

Then again, maybe you are overreacting. Maybe the final product won't have a predominant anti-business bias, and if it does, maybe the board of directors of Conglomerate Enterprises won't object. Besides, a film that has a controversial angle might increase your chances for a network deal, since the networks like films with moral overtones. You learned in film school the importance of S.O.S. (Script, Originality, and Suspense)—and as far as you can tell, this film still has all three. Then again, with a heavily moralistic film, it will be more difficult to obtain general distribution in the theaters, since theater owners try to avoid controversial films whenever possible.

On the other hand, you trust your director's judgment. You certainly don't want to unfairly restrain his creative efforts—especially when you really don't know yet how the whole film will come together. He might not even keep this scene in the film... or perhaps there will be more like it!

Regardless of the quality or merit in what is being created, it differs from the original concept as you had interpreted it in the script. The vision you had for the film has definitely been altered. But perhaps you misjudged the intent of the original script, and the director's vision is equally as valid. After all, you did encourage him to make script changes as he felt appropriate. His changes might very well add to the entertainment value of the final film. In addition, he does seem to be making a stronger statement.

You're torn between confronting the director and not saying anything at all. You think it over and then decide.

YOUR CHOICE

3A Demand immediate changes. See page 28.

3B Voice concerns, suggest revisions to the director. See page 29.

3C Voice concerns, seek revisions by the director. See page 29.

3D Voice concerns only. See page 30.

3E Check on the likely reaction to an anti-business film. See page 30.

3F Wait until the film is closer to being finished. See page 31.

3A Demand immediate changes.

Your director is insulted and shocked. He claims that he thought you both had a common vision for the film and an understanding about your mutual roles. Now you seem to be changing the game plan. He doesn't feel the film has a bias against big business and claims that frank discussions of such matters in the film will raise questions in the minds of the audience, not force answers upon them. The result, he emphatically explains, will be a stronger appreciation for American business and freedom of speech.

He refuses to make any changes. Your attempt is unsuccessful and your concerns are still unresolved.

−2 Points; Choose Again:

YOUR CHOICE

3F Wait until the film is closer to being finished. See page 31.

3G Insist on the changes. See page 32.

3H Drop the issue. See page 32.

3B **Voice concerns, suggest revisions to the director.**

A diplomatic choice. Although you could force the issue and have final say (and you very well may in the future, if need be), you want to seek a resolution which preserves your working relationship with your director. This decision lets you voice your concerns, and provides alternatives for resolution without forcing them on the director. It shows him professional respect and allows him a chance to save face. Of course, you still run the chance that no changes will be made, but you are not 100 percent sure that they need to be.

+3 Points; Please Continue...

Word leaks out to Corporate about the film's bias and you are asked to take action on the matter. What do you do?

YOUR CHOICE

3I Seek changes in the film. See page 33.

3J Defend the film as it is. See page 33.

3K Seek a compromise with Corporate. See page 33.

3C **Voice concerns, seek revisions by the director.**

An excellent choice! Although you could force the issue and have final say (and you still can in the future, if need be), you want to seek a resolution which preserves your working relationship with your director. This decision lets you voice your concerns, and provides alternatives for resolution without forcing them on the director. Soliciting his suggestions for revisions shows your professional respect for him.

+4 Points; Please Continue...

Word leaks out to Corporate about the film's bias and you are asked to take action on the matter. What do you do?

YOUR CHOICE

3I Seek changes in the film. See page 33.

3J Defend the film as it is. See page 33.

3K Seek a compromise with Corporate. See page 33.

3D Voice concerns only.

An acceptable alternative for not infringing upon your director's creative pride. You might not be sending a clear enough message, however, that there will very likely have to be changes made to the film. This could mean additional problems in the future for you. Still, you've brought the potential problem to the director's attention.

+1 Point; Please Continue...

Word leaks out to Corporate about the film's bias and you are asked to take action on the matter. What do you do?

YOUR CHOICE

3I Seek changes in the film. See page 33.

3J Defend the film as it is. See page 33.

3K Seek a compromise with Corporate. See page 33.

3E Check on the likely reaction to an anti-business film.

You bring up your concerns with your manager at Corporate who agrees that it is a risky proposition, one—in fact—with which she would rather not confront upper management. You say you understand and will keep her posted as to progress on the issue. Although she doesn't say anything, you feel she is a bit perturbed that you didn't just handle this matter yourself.

−1 Point; Choose Again:

YOUR CHOICE

3A Demand immediate changes. See page 28.

3B Voice concerns, suggest revisions to the director. See page 29.

3C Voice concerns, seek revisions by the director. See page 29.

3D Voice concerns only. See page 30.

3F Wait until the film is closer to being finished. See below.

3F **Wait until the film is closer to being finished.**

A *big* mistake. This will certainly allow the director's intentions to be clearly expressed in the film; unfortunately, if those intentions differ from your own, not much production time will be left to make the changes that may be needed. If your previous suspicions concerning an unacceptable bias are confirmed, it will have to be edited out, which may leave a choppy, incoherent work. Even worse, costly reshooting may be required.

Communication should be open and ongoing in any intense working relationship. Not bringing up your concerns with Ruckus will *not* make them disappear.

−3 Points; Please Continue...

Word leaks out to Corporate about the film's bias and you are asked to take action on the matter. What do you do?

YOUR CHOICE

3I Seek changes in the film. See page 33.

3J Defend the film as it is. See page 33.

3K Seek a compromise with Corporate. See page 33.

3G Insist on the changes.

You win! Your director backs down and agrees to reshoot the potentially offensive scenes. Fortunately, the scenes to be altered are primarily dialogue, thus making them relatively easy to retake. You definitely bruised your director's feelings, but the film will now be more likely to get the support it will need from Corporate when it hits the market. However, the characters in the film have lost some exposition time in which their motivations for subsequent actions are made clear. As a result, some portions of the film are left hanging—a negative consequence.

+1 Point; Go to Decision #4, page 33.

3H Drop the issue.

A very risky decision. If this is a potential problem, it is likely to get worse before it gets better. Problems are generally easier to resolve when they are smaller and more manageable. Although your director is aware of your concern, he might interpret your not following up on the situation as an acceptance of his expressed position on the matter. When the topic is brought up again at a later date, he might be more firmly committed to his original response, and justifiably upset that you left your expectations on the issue so ambiguous.

−2 Points; Go to Decision #4, page 33.

3I Seek changes in the film.

If you trusted your director, you wouldn't question his judgment.

−2 Points; Go to Decision #4, below.

3J Defend the film as it is.

You should support your director on issues of artistic judgement. Your defense will also help morale on the set.

+2 Points; Go to Decision #4, below.

3K Seek a compromise with Corporate.

Good choice! Explain your strategy for dealing with the director to your superior and explain the importance of handling the situation your way so as to maintain a good relationship with the director.

+2 Points; Go to Decision #4, below.

Decision #4: Overbudget, Behind Schedule

While stuck in rush hour during your morning commute to work, you mentally review the progress of the film's production. Things have been going smoothly on the project for the last few weeks. It is ironic that after mentally congratulating yourself on successfully overcoming some initial difficulties, you walk into your office and find the following memorandum on your desk from the Accounting Department:

CONGLOMERATE ENTERPRISES
MEMORANDUM

It has come to the attention of our department that several line items associated with Project 1407, *Kingdom Come*, will soon be depleted. The next budgeting review cycle for the project is not due to be made until the 7th of next month. We will need appropriate Deviations to Budget request forms with approval by two higher levels of management for the project by week's end if variances are to be honored. Please advise.

Cheryl Brewster

Cheryl Brewster
Accounting Supervisor

This is an unexpected blow! You thought all expenses were being closely monitored by the unit production manager. He's the one that put together the original budget and production schedule. You had not heard from him that funding in certain budget areas was running out. You review the most recent accounting report on the film and call your unit production manager for clarification.

YOU: Just got a notice from accounting. It says we might come up short in a few areas. Do you know anything about this?

PRODUCTION MANAGER: Well it certainly doesn't surprise me! This film was grossly underestimated given the likelihood of the problems we've run into. We've been trying to make do as best we can, but there's a limit to what can be done.

YOU: We went over the budget together—you certainly seemed to think it was reasonable then! You know that the money has got to last this project at least another three weeks. Just exactly how short do you expect to be?

PRODUCTION MANAGER: It's not that easy to say. You know about the problems we had with the last scene—it wasn't working out at all. Well, we thought that changes would add another day, tops, but the director insisted on redoing it until he felt it was perfect. That fiasco alone has set us back three days.

YOU: Are you saying that you don't expect to finish filming by the date we targeted in the revised schedule?

PRODUCTION MANAGER: Until yesterday, I thought we'd be close, but I can hardly see how that will be possible given the recent bad luck we've had. Can't you pull some strings with the budget?

You knew your luck of late on this project was too good to be true. Perhaps you should have been keeping a closer eye on the budget, but you had no reason to think that things were getting out of hand. Although the budget is specifically the unit production manager's responsibility, the director has likely been making it difficult for him to stay within budget because of unreasonable demands on the schedule. What's worse, the production manager seems to have been covering for the director, rarely blaming him for any of the delays or problems. You obtain a copy of the latest project accounting printout and mull over the figures. "Above the line" expenses (which relate to story/script development) are in line, as are most of the fixed percentages (overhead, Actor's Guild, completion fee, and so on). You are having trouble with the "below the line" expenses—especially production costs. That is the section you need to focus on.

Project code: #1407

PRODUCTION BUDGET

Title: *Kingdom Come*

Period: Second quarter

Dollar amounts (in $1,000)

Description	Forecast	Actual	Deviation (+ / −)
Production staff	$255	$299	+ 17%
Extra talent	25	28	+ 12
Art direction	86	97	+ 13
Set construction	29	37	+ 6
Set operations	73	80	+ 10
Camera operations	127	146	+ 15
Sound operations	20	19	− 5
Wardrobe / makeup	37	40	+ 9
Stunts	98	94	− 4
Special effects	152	155	+ 2
Location permits	22	22	—
Transportation	43	52	+ 21
Meals / lodging	144	161	+ 12
Production film and lab	119	151	+ 27
Employee taxes	50	57	+ 17
TOTAL Above-the-Line	$1280	$1438	+ 12%

As expected, the budget is on course for at least a 12 percent cost overrun, if filming is completed on the revised schedule, on time. From the conversation you just had with the production manager, it seems likely that filming will take longer. Some action on your part is obviously needed.

YOUR CHOICE

4A Stop production until the budget problems are resolved. See below.

4B Have the production manager come see you to discuss the situation. See page 38.

4C Visit the set to speak with the production manager. See page 38.

4D Send a subordinate to speak with the production manager. See page 39.

4E Ignore overruns for now. See page 39.

4A Stop all production until the budget concern is resolved.

This will certainly focus attention on the issue! You'll be able to quickly bring the situation under control before it gets worse. Of course, at the same time, it is a drastic and expensive step since many expenses (salaries, rentals, and so on) will continue to be incurred. In addition, momentum that was established on the film will be lost. Your director is also quite likely to view the move as overdramatic and unnecessary, but if it prevents a more serious problem, do you really care? At any rate, he quickly confronts you for an explanation.

+1 Point; Choose Again:

YOUR CHOICE

4F Insist on wrapping up on budget and on schedule. See page 40.

4G Obtain a commitment to a revised budget and schedule. See page 41.

4H Allow leeway in completing the film, but insist on better communication from now on. See page 41.

4B **Have the production manager come see you to discuss the situation.**

Making the production manager come to your office subtly underscores your authority and emphasizes who is working for whom. The meeting is productive.

+2 Points; Please Continue...

The production manager seems to understand your concerns and is willing to make them his priorities. As the meeting draws to a close, you push for an acceptable resolution.

YOUR CHOICE

4F Insist on wrapping up on budget and on schedule. See page 40.

4G Obtain a commitment to a revised budget and schedule. See page 41.

4H Allow leeway in completing the film, but insist on better communication from now on. See page 41.

4C **Visit the set to speak with the production manager.**

Personally seeking additional information through a face-to-face discussion with the production manager shows that you are concerned about the situation. If your tone is not too confrontational, you are likely to obtain the results you desire.

+3 Points, Please Continue...

Unfortunately, the director did not exactly welcome your visit with open arms. In fact, he threw a shoe at you and told you to get off "his" set. Somewhat frustrated, you return to your office to review your options.

Please Choose Again...

YOUR CHOICE

4A Stop all production until the budget concern is resolved. See page 37.

4E Ignore overruns for now. See page 39.

4I Have the production manager hand deliver a letter from you stating you will stop production unless the director contacts you at once to discuss the budget and schedule. See page 41.

4D Send a subordinate to speak with the production manager.

The production manager keeps your subordinate waiting most of the morning. When he does meet with him, he discusses the problem and delivers a list of complaints from the director which concludes with a message to give to you: "Creative excellence demands limitless support. You can't rush genius, so don't try."

This has turned out to be an ineffective way of dealing with an important problem.

−2 Points; Choose Again:

YOUR CHOICE

4A Stop production until the budget concern is resolved. See page 37.

4B Have the production manager come see you to discuss the situation. See page 38.

4C Visit the set to speak with the production manager. See page 38.

4E Ignore overruns for now. See page 39.

4E Ignore overruns for now.

This is a big mistake. What if the director takes forever to finish the film? It could turn out to be another *Apocalypse Now,* or worse yet, *Heavens Gate*—a film that bankrupted the company that produced it.

The latter film had over 17 million feet of film shot and originally included one five-hour battle scene! You have to make sure the tail is not wagging the dog! To ignore the overruns at this point will send a message that the issue is not important to you.

−5 Points; Please Continue . . .

Your superior reviews the progress of the film and is aghast at the overruns. She demands immediate action!

YOUR CHOICE

(Do not select a choice that has been previously made.)

4A Stop production until the budget concern is resolved. See page 37.

4B Have the production manager come see you to discuss the situation. See page 38.

4C Visit the set to speak with the production manager. See page 38.

4I Have the production manager hand deliver a letter from you stating you will stop production unless the director contacts you at once to discuss the budget and schedule. See page 41.

4F Insist on wrapping up on budget and on schedule.

Asserting iron-handed control this far into the project may make you seem authoritarian, inconsistent, and untrusting. You may force the director into making a "cheap wrap" to the film, which is bound to lower the overall quality and thus limit market potential of the film. On the bright side, you'll gain respect from your superiors at Corporate for being an efficient project manager, but then again, their name won't appear on the screen—yours will.

−3 Points; Go to Decision #5, page 42.

4G **Obtain a commitment to a revised budget and schedule.**

This is a good compromise strategy. It will allow you and the director to work together in reestablishing reasonable goals. It will take advantage of considerations you each might have for how to save time and money, while producing an acceptable film with which you can both be proud to be associated.

+3 Points; Go to Decision #5, page 42.

4H **Allow leeway in completing the film, but insist on better communication from now on.**

You are a trusting individual! You gave your crew some leeway before and look at the problems you've had. The situation may soon, however, become a major problem that even you are unable to deal with. You could be removed from the project.

−1 Point; Go to Decision #5, page 42.

4I **Have the production manager hand deliver a letter from you stating you will stop production unless the director contacts you at once to discuss the budget and schedule.**

Your decision choice was both clear and firm. You receive a very pleasant phone call from the director asking if you have time this afternoon to get together. A mutually convenient time is set.

+2 Points; Please Continue . . .

You have a good discussion with the production manager and director which is positive, yet frank about your concerns for the film. The director's tone is pleasant and cooperative, and you feel that he both understands and sees the merit in your concerns. As the conversation winds down, you push for an acceptable resolution.

YOUR CHOICE

4E Insist on wrapping up on budget and on schedule. See page 39.

4F Obtain a commitment to a revised budget and schedule. See page 40.

4G Allow leeway in completing the film, but insist on better communication from now on. See page 41.

4J Ignore overruns for now. See page 42.

4J Ignore overruns for now.

Problems do not usually go away by themselves. By dropping the issue at this point, you may not know if the director and production manager clearly understand the problem or are capable of coming up with an acceptable resolution. Although you may be trying to show your trust in your staff, you do not want to extend a blind faith. After all, you have already been unpleasantly surprised on this project, why take an unnecessary risk?

You need to establish some clearer rules for the continued progress of the film.

−2 Points; Continue to Decision #5, page 42.

Decision #5: Market Research

Production on the film is winding down and you begin to prepare for the film's release. You consult with the marketing research department to discuss the film's promotion campaign. They were involved in the initial evaluation of the film's market potential many months earlier, and their role now will be specifically to help plan a marketing strategy based upon the unique "handles" that the film has. A market analyst is giving you a report of recent findings...

MARKET ANALYST: The market for high-action films is definitely glutted right now, so we need to minimize that aspect of the film. *Kingdom Come* has more plot than most releases, but emphasizing that fact may cause it to look too highbrow.

YOU: You're telling me approaches we shouldn't take, what about approaches we should take?

MARKET ANALYST: Sorry. I don't mean to be negative because I really like this film. It's just that the demographics of the industry have shifted dramatically in the last decade, and a film of this quality is more difficult to release as a result.

YOU: How do you mean?

MARKET ANALYST: Well, take a look at this chart. It shows the demographic shift I'm referring to.

THEATER ATTENDANCE BY AGE GROUP

Age	1975	1980	1985
Below 11	3%	2%	7%
11-15	15	23	34
16-20	21	19	27
21-25	22	27	17
26-30	23	17	8
31-35	7	4	5
36-40	4	4	2
41-45	3	5	*
46-50	*	*	1
Over 50	1	*	*
TOTALS**	99%	101%	100%

*less than one percent reported

**totals may not equal 100% due to rounding off

MARKET ANALYST: There is an undeniable shift to a younger viewing audience in large part due to the widespread acceptance of the VCR. Over 40 percent of American homes now have one, and the convenience of watching a movie at home and the increased selection that is available for the home market has had an enormous impact on film releases. People still go to the movies, but the reasons why are changing.

YOU: What are those reasons?

MARKET ANALYST: Well, there is less urgency to see a film when it is first released since it will likely be a rental within a year, if not sooner. Marketing efforts have to convince potential viewers that the film is so good they don't want to wait. Of course there's still a certain attraction to seeing a film with a large group, smelling the aroma of popcorn, getting a chance to get out of the house, and so on. For the younger viewers, going to the movies is still a very social activity—a chance to see friends and a place to take a date.

YOU: You're making me think I'm in the wrong business.

MARKET ANALYST: I don't mean to sound gloomy, I just want us to be realistic in our approach. People still go to the movies—just different people than a decade ago. In fact, the number of Americans who go to the movies has increased in the last few years. Here's a breakdown by frequency:

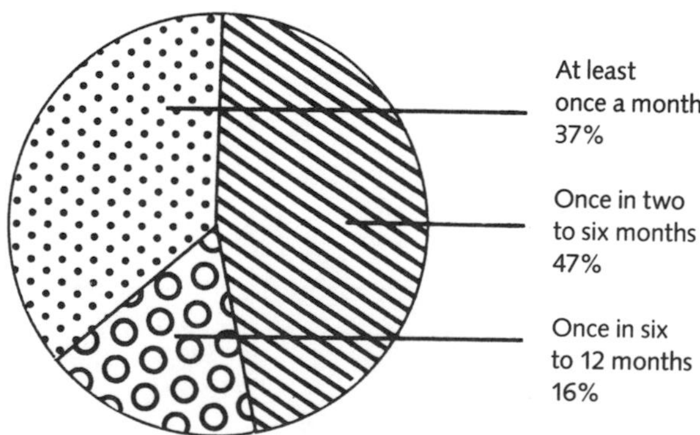

MARKET ANALYST: A film aimed at an older market such as this one is can still be enormously successful, especially if it were to gain the attention of the Academy, for example.

YOU: How were the previews received?

MARKET ANALYST: The previews in our test markets were very favorably received. From our advertising, which we intentionally kept a bit ambigious, people weren't sure what to expect, but in general they enjoyed the film and over 70 percent said they would recommend it to a friend. If that statistic holds up in a general release we could have a groundswell of support.

YOU: Based on all of this, do you have a recommended approach to releasing this film?

MARKET ANALYST: Yes, as we discussed this film in our department, it was generally agreed that timing would be a crucial element in this film's release. With a strong word-of-mouth potential, we think it's important to release the film during one of the two "big release" periods of the year—either Christmas or summer—in order to maximize its sales potential, with our preference being the Christmas season since that tends to bring out an older audience.

YOU: That would mean delaying the release date by six to eight months from our original schedule.

MARKET ANALYST: That's right.

Your gut reaction is that waiting will not significantly affect the film's chances of success. You are likely to have more competition during a peak viewing season, especially from films of a similar genre, but statistics show that people go to more movies during the holidays, so you could still have a big draw. You believe that there may, in fact, be a greater risk involved in waiting since the market is unpredictable. The film might receive a cooler reception six to eight months in the future than it would if released as scheduled, especially if it does, in fact, have a "groundswell" potential. Advice from marketing research has had little correlation with how successful a film ultimately is, although you feel a certain obligation to make use of the data they have painstakingly collected. For now, you need to decide whether or not to accept the advice you just received from the marketing analyst.

YOUR CHOICE

5A Reject the advice, release film as originally planned. See below.

5B Accept the advice, wait six to eight months before releasing the film. See below.

5A Reject the advice, release film as originally planned.

Preliminary response to the film in its first week has been strong, suggesting that the film will be successful!

Advice is just that—no one knows the future for certain. Following your instincts may seem risky and unscientific, but in this case it seems as though it might pay off. As long as you have objectively weighed the pros and cons of the advice, and the track record of those who are providing the advice, you can feel good about your decision. Besides, you've come a long way with this project based upon your belief in it. If you wanted a sure thing, you'd be in a different line of work!

You'll never know for sure if you made the best decision. If the film ultimately fails, the marketing research department will say they told you so. If it succeeds, they'll say it would have done better had it been released when they advised. In this case, you seem to have lucked out.

+2 Points; Go to Decision #6, page 47.

5B Accept the advice, wait six to eight months before releasing the film.

It feels like a bad dream, one of the competing studios released a similar film to *Kingdom Come* several months ahead of schedule. It's difficult to be certain, but it seems likely that they will cut into the audience share you hoped to get. Some reviewers are even claiming that your film is a knock-off of the film that was released first!

Quantitative analysis may appear to be exact and precise, but in this industry, it never is. You should use numbers to double check your instincts, not to form them.

You'll still never know for sure if you made the best decision. If the film fails, the marketing research department might claim it was because of other factors they didn't or couldn't predict. If the film succeeds, it might have done just as well—or even better—if it had been released earlier. In this instance, however, you will probably lose sales...

–2 Points; Go to Decision #6, below.

Decision #6: Distribution and Promotion

The film is released on a limited basis and after several weeks the reviews have been mixed and inconsistent. A typical exerpt:

Kingdom Come Has Some Moments, But Too Few

by Rex Snead

This new release by Amalgamated Films shows strong creative effort and daring. The film has the potential to blow you away, but somehow doesn't quite deliver in the final analysis.

The plot is involved, and at times complex, and although the acting is excellent, members of the audience are left scratching their heads as a twist of events is not quite believable or secondary characters behave in inconsistent ways...

Reviewers' comments are matched by distributors' reactions. Since the film is not easily categorized (for instance, action-adventure, comedy, political thriller, social satire), many distributors are unsure how to handle it, if at all. Theater chains indicate a resistance to carry the film for extensive national distribution or for a guaranteed run length. You have a number of strategies you can follow, and you consider the pros and cons of each:

Withdraw and reedit the film. A potentially expensive alternative, but one which could alleviate some of the perceived inconsistencies in the film. *The Big Chill,* for example, had the final scene (a lengthy flashback) cut out after test audiences expressed confusion. You might, however, be compromising the unique nature of the film by being over-anxious to please reviewers and distributors.

Reevaluate promotional angles. You can redefine your promotional campaign to more specifically target a certain market segment. You can appeal directly to the consumer through a promotional blitz and thus attempt to negate or preempt negative reviews. Such a commitment would also indicate to distributors that you strongly believe in the film and they will be more likely to carry it. *The Deep* had well-coordinated hype in just such a manner. Since the story line did not have the draw of *Jaws,* the promotion strategy sought to saturate the market before the general viewing public realized the film was mediocre at best. Instead of just releasing the film in big theaters and letting it filter out to smaller ones (a typical progression), the film was released to a much greater number of theaters. The book was hyped, yet copies were not made available until immediatedly preceeding the film's release (so that it would not be possible to read the book and decide the film wasn't worth seeing). On the other hand, you may be pouring money into a loser and end up incurring greater losses than you would have otherwise.

Continue promotions as planned. Continue with your original promotions plan, which involves a steady advertising campaign, ignoring the mixed reactions from reviewers. If you persevere in your original plan, the merits of the film may carry it in the market as the film attains greater audience exposure. It might even become an adult-oriented "cult" film, perhaps like *My Dinner with André.*

Drop promotions in an effort to cut your losses. This will definitely be the path of least resistance, given the ambiguous reaction you have encountered to date. Print and ad budgets are frequently altered based upon the initial responses in the market. After all, a studio cannot get behind every single film it produces—resources are too limited.

YOUR CHOICE

6A Withdraw and reedit the film. See below.

6B Reevaluate promotional angles. See below.

6C Continue promotions as planned. See page 50.

6D Drop promotions in an effort to cut your losses. See page 50.

6A Withdraw and reedit the film.

The film is now clearer, but unfortunately it has lost most of its intrigue as well, and the reviews turn consistently negative.

−4 Points; Please Continue . . .

You feel compelled to take some action. Which do you prefer:

YOUR CHOICE

6D Drop promotions in an effort to cut your losses. See page 50.

6E Conduct a promotional blitz. See page 51.

6B Reevaluate promotional angles.

It is good to be responsive to reactions in the marketplace! Some change in strategy is in order, and your choice is probably the most cost effective at this stage of release.

+3 Points; Please Continue . . .

What change in promotions would you like to make?

YOUR CHOICE

6E Conduct a promotional blitz. See page 51.

6F More specifically target one segment of the market. See page 51.

6C **Continue promotions as planned.**

Sticking to a plan has some merit, but it's a good idea to integrate new information as you get it and change the plan accordingly.

−1 Point; Please Continue…

Continued promotions produce no noticable change in audience attendance. What do you propose to do?

YOUR CHOICE

6D Drop promotions in an effort to cut your losses. See page 50.

6E Conduct a promotional blitz. See page 51.

6D **Drop promotions in an effort to cut your losses.**

You saved some money on promotions but audience attendance immediately dropped. The film makes an early close.

−2 Points; Please Continue…

You could attempt to revive the film with a promotional blitz (although it would be costly) or instead try to make up your losses in the subsidiary markets.

YOUR CHOICE

6E Conduct a promotional blitz. See below.

6G Try to recoup losses in subsidiary markets. See page 52.

6E Conduct a promotional blitz.

If you really believe in this movie, you need to be willing to take some risks. A promotional blitz will help to sell the general viewing public, and since you have evidence that 70 percent of viewers are likely to recommend the film to others, this looks like it will be a sound investment.

+4 Points; Please Go to Decision #7, page 53.

6F More specifically target one segment of the market.

With success in a targeted market, you will have a proven track record that will persuade distributors to carry the film on a more widespread basis.

+3 Points; Please Continue . . .

There are two main ways to target segments of a movie audience. You can focus all promotions on a specific age group in an attempt to increase film identification by that age group. You can also "four-wall" the film, that is, buy viewing time in a number of theaters in a specific geographical area and then follow the market with a print and ads campaign.

What type of market segment would you like to target?

YOUR CHOICE

6H An "age group" market segment. See below.

6I A "geographical" market segment. See below.

6G **Try to recoup losses in subsidiary markets.**

This would have been much easier to do if there had been adequate promotion!

−2 Points; Go to Decision #7, page 53.

6H **Target an "age group" market segment.**

This film's appeal is too nebulous and such an approach will not work well. If *Kingdom Come* were a horror film or primarily action-adventure, you could successfully target a junior-high group. Such targeting will be much more difficult to do with this film, however.

−1 Point; Please Go to Decision #7, page 53.

6I **Target a "geographical" market segment.**

This can be an effective approach in promoting *Kingdom Come,* because impressive results in a specific georaphical market (especially if it's a major market) can give you influence in distribution of the film into other regional markets and with larger distributors.

+1 Point; Please Go to Decision #7, page 53.

DECISION #7: ANCILLARY MARKETS

Subsidiary markets have increasingly gained importance in the film industry as a means for making a profit on a movie. In some instances a box office flop can become a success due to the growing demand for films in such markets. *Kingdom Come* is due out shortly on a nation-wide basis. Although it is still too early to tell how successful it will be, you have had several discussions with representatives of the networks, cable, syndication, home video, and overseas subsidiary markets concerning subsidiary rights to the film, which you have retained. All parties have expressed an interest in the film, although the proposed offers vary tremendously. Alternatives need to be systematically evaluated and compared to obtain the highest possibility for maximum profits. You seek the assistance of Amalgamated's agent for rights transactions to discuss the various offers:

YOU: It's still unclear how *Kingdom Come* will ultimately fare in the theaters, so we want to do the most to try to recoup our investment in the secondary market.

RIGHTS AGENT: The fact that the film's success is still an unknown can work to our favor in selling the rights since its potential is still high. Of course, if we think it might still break out, it would be to our advantage to wait until a positive track record is established for the film.

YOU: What would be the normal order of events?

RIGHTS AGENT: Increasingly, we are preselling films for specific markets that have paid for a percentage of the film costs prior to production. With this film, however, it is to our advantage to have a finished product. Traditionally, a new release would first come out in the theaters; three months or so later it would be released in the home video market; after another four months or so it would be seen on cable TV; and a year later, on the networks. That pattern, however, can vary tremendously depending upon such variables as how successful the film is expected to be, the topic and genre of the film, the ease or difficulty in obtaining distribution, and whether exclusivity is required by the purchasing party.

YOU: Exclusivity seems to be a primary concern only for the network and cable markets.

RIGHTS AGENT: It would be to our advantage to negotiate a number of deals rather than to be locked into just one secondary market. Unless we had an exceptional deal from a single secondary market vehicle, we would be more likely to produce a more desirable income stream by negotiating several deals. Let's see what offers you have and then decide which is the best deal.

YOU: Here's a run down on the terms, pros and cons of the deals I can likely get:

Network offer. "The networks like this film because it has a controversial theme. We could get $2 million up front for two exclusive viewing "windows," usually one 12- to 18-month period. They would show the film once per major viewing season (fall and spring). The network exposure is good unless so many people see the film on TV that all other market potential is lost. The exclusive period prevents other deals, thus we lose advantage of the initial promotional effort for the movie."

Cable TV offer. "Cable is always trying to offer exclusive showings, although after they have shown the film first on television, they do not care who else shows it in subsequent seasons (after a six-month period). We could likely get $1 million plus $250,000 per additional showing, which would be at least several times during the year and—if the film is well-rated by their subscribers—additional times in subsequent years."

Syndication. "This is a rapidly expanding secondary market that services the growing number of independent television stations across the country. This market is starved for product, so deals can be easily made. They would pay us slightly less than the cable market ($750,000), but offer a percentage of the subscriber's fee they collect, probably around 20 percent of gross revenues. Of course, once they have shown the film, neither the networks or cable will be interested in it for some time."

Home video offer. "There seems to be an insatiable demand for new videos! We could get a flat $3.5 million, which is on the high end as video deals go, but with no royalty percentage. There is also no exclusivity requirement, in fact, the current preference in this market is to carry films that have already been successful in other markets, especially the U.S. theatrical market, although there is talk that soon companies such as Vestron, CBS, and Media Home Entertainment will be advertising films that will not be shown in theaters or on television, and will only be available from video rental stores. Deals in this market are becoming increasingly more lucrative."

Overseas offer. "The overseas market tends to have a bias toward action-oriented American films. We could get a $500,000 advance against 50 percent of gross receipts, which could likely add up to several million dollars in the first few years. No exclusivity would be required."

There is quite a lot of interest in the film which is, of course, good. There are other deals that can be made (books, licensing, posters) depending upon how successful the film is. For right now you just want to compare and contrast the various offers already described to see which you most prefer. You make a simple chart to assist with your decision.

PENDING SUBSIDIARY OFFERS

(in $1000s)

Offer	Terms	Comments
Network	$2000 for two windows	12-month exclusive
Cable	$1000 + $250 / showing	6-month exclusive
Syndication	$750 + 20% of gross	Growing market
Home video market	$3500 + no royalty	Explosive market
Overseas	$500 + 50% of gross	Strong demand, no exclusivity

Which is your first choice for a subsidiary deal?

YOUR CHOICE

7A Accept the network offer. See page 56.

7B Accept the cable TV offer. See page 56.

7C Accept the syndication offer. See page 57.

7D Accept the home video offer. See page 57.

7E Accept the overseas offer. See page 58.

7A Accept the network offer.

A marginal choice. You will increase the film's exposure which should increase its long-range earnings potential, but you will also have to limit your dealings in other markets for 12 months, which will minimize the effect of current advertising and promotions.

−2 Points; Please Continue...

The cable market is still interested in the film, although the upfront money would be $500,000 less. Other offers remain the same. What is your second choice of offers?

YOUR CHOICE

7F Accept the cable TV offer at $500,000 less. See page 59.

7G Accept the home video offer. See page 59.

7H Accept the overseas offer. See page 59.

7B Accept the cable TV offer.

Although the upfront money is substantially lower than the network or home video offers, cable will show the film many more times than the networks, and the exclusivity period is shorter, allowing you to make some other deals while the film is being heavily promoted.

+2 Points; Please Continue...

Bonus points: Added exposure of the film enables you to get a better deal! If you had previously conducted a promotional blitz for this film (Decision Selection 6E), **add a bonus +3 points to your score.**

Although the networks and syndication are no longer interested in the film, what would be your second choice for a subsidiary market deal?

YOUR CHOICE

7H Accept the overseas offer. See page 59.

7I Accept the home video offer. See page 59.

7C **Accept the syndication offer.**

This is a poor choice for initially maximizing the exposure for the film. However, royalty terms are more lucrative since syndicators are hungry for products.

−3 Points; Please Continue...

The networks are no longer interested in the film although the cable market will still consider it for a lower advance. What is your second preference for a subsidiary deal?

YOUR CHOICE

7F Accept the cable TV offer at $500,000 less. See page 59.

7G Accept the home video offer. See page 59.

7H Accept the overseas offer. See page 59.

7D **Accept the home video offer.**

In today's market, this is probably your best deal. It nets you the most money up front, although you are diminishing your long-range profitability by not making a deal in the cable or network markets. Your greatest visibility for video sales is in the theatrical market with a good print and ads campaign and good reviews. You could have possibly gotten a higher amount in this market after the film had been shown on television and more people knew about it. But since 40 percent of American homes have a VCR, you are definitely with the viewing trend. After all, if a family can see a film at home for $2–3 dollars, they have a great incentive not to go out to see a film for $20–25.

+4 Points; Please Continue...

Bonus points: Added exposure of the film enables you to get a better deal! If you had previously conducted a promotional blitz for this film (Decision Selection 6E), **add +3 bonus points to your score.**

Athough the networks are no longer interested in the film, you can still get an offer in the cable market, but at $250,000 less than an exclusive offer would have obtained. What is your second subsidiary market choice?

YOUR CHOICE

7H Accept the overseas offer. See page 59.

7J Accept the cable TV offer at $250,000 less. See page 60.

7K Accept the syndication offer. See page 60.

7E **Accept the overseas offer.**

The overseas market can potentially be much larger than the U.S. theatrical market especially for a film that has a fair degree of action. After all, many countries with extensive theater systems have not yet been infiltrated with VCRs. Although this deal will not affect the exclusivity of the film in the American market, it probably is not the best initial choice, because the upfront money is lower and you gain no additional exposure in the U.S. market.

+2 Points; Please Continue...

Bonus points: Special effects are currently quite popular abroad! If you emphasized special effects in Decision #1 (Decision Selections 1B, 1N, or 1W) **add +3 points to your score.**

Please choose again:

7I Accept the home video offer. See page 60.

7L Accept the network offer. See page 60.

7M Accept the cable TV offer. See page 61.

7F **Accept the cable TV offer at $500,000 less.**

You are winding down available options instead of taking advantage of opportunities while the film is being more heavily promoted.

−2 Points; Go to "Case Analysis," page 62.

7G **Accept the home video offer.**

Since you already sold the rights to a network or syndication, the film has been widely seen and demand is greatly reduced in the home video market.

−2 Points; Go to "Case Analysis," page 62.

7H **Accept the overseas offer.**

You could always negotiate an overseas offer after the film has had wider exposure in the U.S., but it is a strong market for the film.

+2 Points; Please Continue...

Bonus points: Special effects are currently quite popular abroad! If you emphasized special effects in Decision #1 (Decision Selections 1B, 1N, or 1W), **add +3 points to your score.**

Go to "Case Analysis," page 62.

7I **Accept the home video offer.**

Still a strong choice, especially given the upfront money.

+3 Points; Go to "Case Analysis," page 62.

7J **Accept the cable TV offer at $250,000 less.**

An acceptable offer, although certainly not as attractive as the initial cable offer.

+1 Point; Go to "Case Analysis," page 62.

7K **Accept the syndication offer.**

You probably could have done better with another offer for more money and better exposure.

−3 Points; Go to "Case Analysis," page 62.

7L **Accept the network offer.**

You have limited other potential deals on this film for 12 months, and thus will not be able to take advantage of promotions at the time of the film's release.

−2 Points; Go to "Case Analysis," page 62.

7M **Accept the cable TV offer.**

This is is still a strong offer. Although you could have gotten more upfront money, you will be able to make other deals after six months.

+3 Points; Go to "Case Analysis," page 62.

Results of Film Release: Case Analysis

Kingdom Come has finally been released throughout the country. To see how well the film did, total the number of points you scored from all your decisions and turn to the page indicated.

+45 points or more. See R1, below.

+30 to +44 points. See R2, page 63.

+20 to +29 points. See R3, page 63.

−19 to +19 points. See R4, page 63.

−20 to −34 points. See R5, page 64.

−35 points or below. See R6, page 64.

R1: Blockbuster (+45 points or more.)

Film grosses $100 million plus! You get promoted; the director buys you a Mercedes!

You always secretly suspected this film would break out big. Good decision making and a little (or a lot) of luck made it happen—congratulations! Send your résumé with salary requirements to: MGM Studios, 10202 West Washington Blvd., Culver City, CA 90232.

It is difficult to know exactly why a film succeeds, but you most likely made several decisions which helped the film's odds in the market. To gain additional insight into which decisions most likely made the difference, see:

"Decision Analysis," page 65.

"Probable Reasons for the Film's Success," page 67.

R2: Successful (+30 to +44 points.)

Film grosses over $50 million! You get a raise and a bonus!

You beat the odds and had to make some good decisions to do it. It is difficult to know exactly why a film succeeds, but you most likely made several decisions which helped the film's odds in the market. For additional insight into which decisions made an impact, see:

"Decision Analysis," page 65.

"Probable Reasons for the Film's Success," page 67.

R3: Breakeven (+20 to +29 points.)

Film earns back sunk costs; you keep your job.

You earned back the money this film cost to produce and market. To do so you had to make a few "correct" decisions along the way. For additional insight into which decisions were most beneficial, see:

"Decision Analysis," page 65.

"Probable Reasons for the Film's Success," page 67.

R4: Film Fails (−19 to +19 points.)

Your year-end bonus is cancelled.

Ah, the fickle viewing public! The film is panned by the critics and no one goes to see it. Perhaps you caught the audience at the wrong time. You might have thought you had the pulse of the nation just right and the trends changed. Perhaps costs got out of hand, making it almost impossible for this film to make a profit. Perhaps nothing you could have done would have mattered anyway. Although you heard various rumors attributing failure to different reasons, failure is rarely due to a single factor, and you'll never know for sure what went wrong.

If you selected Choice 6E or 7D, go to R7, page 64.

For additional rationale as to the scoring of decision selections, see:

"Decision Analysis," page 65.

"Probable Reason for the Film's Failure," page 69.

R5: FILM FAILS (−20 to −34 points.)

You are fired!

Better luck next time. Hopefully, you are only paying your dues for what will become a phenomonenal career. For additional insight into your poor fortune see:

"Decision Analysis," page 65.

"Probable Reasons for the Film's Failure," page 69.

R6: FILM BOMBS (−35 points or below.)

You are fired and the film company goes bankrupt.

Take a six-month cruise to recuperate and forget. For additional insight into your poor fortune see:

"Decision Analysis," page 65.

"Probable Reasons for the Film's Failure," page 69.

R7: SLEEPER (−19 to +19 points, plus Choice 6E or 7D.)

Film initially fails, but succeeds in the long run.

You beat the odds and the reviewers! They panned the film when it was released, but the public eventually came through for you. Fortunately, you stuck with the film, even at times when it seemed certain you had a dog on your hands.

For additional insight into scoring see:

"Decision Analysis," page 65.

"Probable Reasons for Film Becoming a Late Success," page 72.

RESULTS OF FILM RELEASE: DECISION ANALYSIS

Here is a brief summary of what you had to do (and why) to obtain the optimal score for each decision.

DECISION #1: BUDGET ALLOCATION

To obtain the maximum points for this decision you had to have an understanding of what factors are most crucial to the success of a film, and consistently select elements that would enhance this film's success. Putting your money on name talent was the best choice, especially if you were able to skillfully negotiate a better financial deal than was initially offered. If you didn't stress talent, special effects were the next best approach for investing. A strong promotions budget could have helped the film if you had emphasized talent or special effects, otherwise the money most likely would have been wasted. A high-quality script was only an advantage if you had good acting talent to use it, otherwise that too was wasted money. Good music was always a plus.

DECISION #2: DIRECTOR PERKS

This issue clearly had significant emotional implications and possible status repercussions, but the financial cost was actually quite minimal ($50,000 on a $23+ million budget). To establish and preserve a good working relationship with the director you needed to give him clear support. If you were able to mediate the clash without alienating your corporate superiors or, more importantly, your director, you received maximum points.

DECISION #3: ETHICS AND ARTISTIC MERIT

Once again, you needed to support the person you hired for his skills (the director) in an effective and diplomatic way. It was important to take action and treat the issue as a high priority, but ideally without unilaterally dictating a solution. Ideally, you explained your concerns and encouraged the director to make revisions of his choosing to the film. You needed to maintain a strong working relationship with your director, even if it meant ignoring your corporate superior at times so as to avoid unnecessary conflict.

Decision #4: Overbudget, Behind Schedule

This is a frequent and significant problem in the film business! It was important for you to take a stand on this issue and persist until the director acknowledged and agreed to keep costs within a reasonable budget. If a compromise was not forthcoming, progressively more authoritarian action on your part was necessary to effectively carry out your responsibilities and keep the project from becoming too expensive.

Decision #5: Marketing Research

Although you may at times be wrong, this is a business in which success is made on hunches. The highest score favored following your instincts.

Decision #6: Distribution and Promotion

You needed to make the best of a troublesome film. In this case, the highest scores were rewarded to aggressive approaches in handling the potentially disastrous situation of early unfavorable reviews. Attempts to manipulate the viewing public through targeted marketing or promotional blitzing, if selected, enabled you to significantly increase the film's chances of commercial success in the market place. Of course, this strategy will not necessarily work for every film, but it worked for this one!

Decision #7: Ancillary Markets

How you handled the issue of subsidiary market deals could have, in itself, turned the tables to make an unprofitable film a commercial success. You wanted to obtain the greatest dollars and exposure (which could translate into other deals as the film became better known). You needed to be sensitive and somewhat aware of the effects of widespread adoption of videocassette players in the American marketplace. Decisions reflecting the expansive clout of the video market were most rewarded, as were those reflecting the potential of the overseas market. These two deals required no exclusivity agreement and thus allowed you to make other deals while the film was receiving heavy initial promotion.

Probable Reasons for the Film's Success

Most likely the film was successful due to a combination of the following factors and decision selections that you made.

Issue / Choice Number	Comments
QUALITY	
1H, 1I, 1R, 1T	Getting name talent helped to assure a high-quality film. (In addition, if you picked Decision Selection 1V, your improved script really helped.)
1C, 1J	A quality soundtrack was a good place to invest!
1B, 1N	Special effects helped this film, especially if you also picked Choice 1K (extra marketing and promotion) or Choices 7E or 7H (an overseas subsidiary deal).
3B, 3C, 3D, 3J, 3K, 4H	You were wise to allow the director leeway for artistic merit—that's what you hired him for!
PROMOTION	
1L	You had the right elements in your film to benefit from added promotions.
3G	Your changes helped gain the support of top management who subsequently agreed to more heavily promote the film.
6E	A promotional blitz was just what the film needed to make it go in the market.
6F	It was a good idea to focus your marketing to build a strong track record for the film.
7A, 7B, 7G, 7L, 7M	These choices gave the film maximum exposure in the market; exposure you will be able to trade on in other subsidiary deals.

TIMING	
5A	It was wise to go with your instincts and release the film when it was initially ready.
COSTS	
4A, 4F, 4G	You kept costs under control when they were on the verge of getting out of hand.
7A, 7D, 7G, 7L	These choices allowed you to recoup your initial investment as soon as possible (although other choices might have made the film more financially successful in the long run).

Please continue to Case #2, page 73.

Probable Reasons for the Film's Failure

The film's failure was due, most likely, to quality, poor promotion, poor timing, or excessive costs. You'll never know for sure, but these were likely the contributing factors to the film's poor performance:

Issue / Choice Number	Comments
POOR QUALITY	
1K, 1Q	The story line and action didn't carry the film—a big name might have helped. You shouldn't have settled for a lesser talent!
2E	The new director didn't do the job you had hoped for—you perhaps should have been more lenient with the original director who most likely could have produced a higher quality product.
3A	You got your desired changes, but the final film was somewhat choppy as a result. Your approach alienated the director and cast when they needed your support; morale and motivation were hampered as a result.
4A	You probably overreacted to the initial indicators you had. The film stayed within budget, but the ending was prematurely shortened and the few people who did see the film were disappointed.
POOR PROMOTION	
1O	You didn't have strong enough elements in this film to warrant the promotions activity you conducted. The money was wasted.
3D, 3F, 3H	You gave the director too much freedom and when the final product was unacceptable to Corporate, it was too late and too expensive to make the changes they wanted. They elected instead to release the film but not promote it.

6D	You cut your losses, but word did not successfully get out about the film and revenues suffered as well.
TIMING	
2G	When your first director quit, the delay really threw off the timing of the project.
3F	When you waited to make suggestions, you seriously crimped the buffer time of the project.
5B	Those folks in marketing research seemed to know what they were talking about, but the fact of the matter is no one can predict the future with accuracy. Delaying the release of the film may have changed its prospects from bad to worse.
6A	Your additional efforts to reedit the film cost several months. Although you didn't know it at the time, your film missed the tail end of an audience viewing trend.
7A, 7C, 7K, 7L	A network or syndication offer gave you little leverage for making other rights deals.
7E, 7H	You failed to take advantage of the film's domestic promotional activities when you made an overseas subsidiary offer a priority for the film.
EXCESSIVE COSTS	
1H, 1U, 1X	You had some name talent, but you paid too much for it.
1K, 1O, 1W	These activities turned out to be ineffective given the nature of the film. The money spent was essentially wasted.
1M	You were too hesitant in budgeting money where it was needed the most.

4H	Your commitment to allow the director to finish the film as he initially intended was akin to writing a blank check. The finished film was of exceptional quality and is likely to become a classic, but it won't pay for itself for over ten years—if then.
4E, 4J	Ignoring overruns can be a costly error!
7B, 7F, 7H, 7J	You didn't get much upfront money on these subsidiary deals!

Please continue to Case #2, page 73.

Probable Reasons for the Film Becoming a Late Success

It seems your luck might have been influenced by one or both of the following selections:

Issue / Choice Number	Comments
PROMOTIONAL BLITZ	
6E	A promotional blitz was a risky decision, but it paid off in this case. The increased promotions generated a greater audience awareness about the film which translated into increased attendance. It also showed distributors and others in the industry that you were serious about this movie, thus enabling you to make some profitable subsidiary deals.
SUBSIDIARY DEAL	
7D	The home video market offer provided you with good upfront money and exposure. The film became so popular it was rereleased to an expanded market by the studio and later shown on several networks—activities that produced welcome added revenues.

Please continue to Case #2, page 73.

CASE #2

Regala Star Consulting Company, Inc.

BRIEFING

Consulting is a fast-paced, demanding profession. Deadlines are constant and the pressure to meet them is intense. Long hours are the norm. But consulting can also be a rewarding profession. Consultants excel at helping corporate clients with key problems, and in the process, they interact with executives on an equal footing. The job is stimulating and challenging. Consultants must constantly learn and integrate new information about different industries, markets, and technical processes. A year of consulting experience is generally considered comparable to three years of industry experience because of the exposure to different problems and situations. For their efforts, consultants are paid well—$50,000 to $90,000 per year on the average—and enjoy a wide latitude of independence.

INDUSTRY DESCRIPTION

There are estimated to be over fifty thousand practicing consultants in the United States, approximately seventeen thousand of whom are employed by the top thirty consulting firms. The remainder are in-house corporate consultants and college and university professors who participate in the profession on a part-time basis. The total market for consulting services is estimated to be about $3 billion a year, which tends to be evenly divided among three sectors of the consulting profession: consulting divisions of the large public accounting firms, which range in size from $50 to 175 million in annual revenues; large independent consulting firms; and smaller independent consulting firms. Independent and part-time consultants, although significant in number, make up a marginal portion of the total consulting market.

Firm Description

Regala Star is an independent firm of about 25 employees which initially specialized in the aeronautics industry over nine years ago, but which now serves a wide variety of client needs in several unrelated industries. The firm has marketing niches in several technical areas of expertise, but also works in nontechnical areas such as management consulting. A large share of the firm's business is repeat or "add-on" business with existing clients. Gross revenues for the firm in the last fiscal year exceeded $3 million. Partners in the firm are active in a wide range of community affairs and often give presentations to boost the image and prestige of the firm to potential clients in the hopes of obtaining new business.

Reader Role

You are a senior partner who has been with Regala Star Consulting Company for seven years. Prior to joining the firm, you worked for five years in line management at a large computer company, where you had manufacturing responsibilities in the production of microprocessors. You later earned an MBA from Columbia University. Your speciality when you joined the firm was organizational behavior and analysis (for which you are still consulted), although now your most important responsibilities at Regala Star involve bringing in additional business with both new and existing clients. You have a good reputation for having specific expertise, intelligence, and managerial and administrative abilities, as well as an ability to please clients (which you attribute to your commitment to service). You do not get too closely involved with the day-to-day details of most projects. You do, however, have ultimate responsibility for the success of those jobs you sell, and you tend to pay closer attention to progress on the larger projects for which you have responsibility. You spend a fair portion of your time with quality assurance: managing those who are doing the work necessary to fulfill the contract, making sure that the products or deliverables meet the agreed-upon specifications, and making sure the client is satisfied both during and after the project.

DECISION #1: NEW CONTRACT BID

"Do you have a minute?" George says, as he pulls you aside at the monthly meeting of the Financial Investors Association.

"George! Good to see you! How's the accounting business treating you?"

"Can't complain. I've been working for the Simex Corporation, helping the accounting department with their year-end closing. Between you and me, they have been having a tough go of it lately."

"So I've heard. What seems to be the problem?"

"It's hard to say for sure. They just had a new product introduction completely bomb, and they're worried about losing market share in some of their traditional product line. They're looking to bring some expertise in to help them out. In fact, they're having a prebid contract meeting this week that you should try to get in on."

"That sounds great. Do you have a contact for me?"

"Here's a name and a number; give me a few days to tell them about you."

"Fine. I owe you one."

This is just the news you needed today. You've wanted to break into Simex for several years. You return to your office and buzz a research associate on the intercom:

"Michele, see what you can find out about recent developments at Simex. Check all the current affairs media, industry analyst reports, and have a look at their 10K and annual report. See what you can give me by tomorrow."

The next morning when you get to work there is a one page summary on top of a stack of newspaper clippings, papers, and brochures on your desk. The top clipping is from the business section of the local paper, dated three months previously:

SIMEX INTRODUCES NEW PERIPHERAL

The Simex Corporation today announced the introduction of a new laser printer designed to set a new industry standard. A spokesperson for the firm expressed optimism about the new product and its prospects in the market. Besides being faster than previous laser printers currently made by the company, this printer contains several engineering advances never before seen in the industry...

Several days later you call the contact you were given and find out that an informal prebid meeting is scheduled, and you get the time and place. (Prebid meetings are most commonly held for large contracts, an indicator to you that this job might be tied to additional work.) You decide to show up early to the meeting to get a feel for the competition.

The room has about 30 people in it, most of them aged 25 to 35, and all dressed conservatively. Glancing about at name tags, you conclude that about eight firms are represented. Those present include the usual assortment of representatives from the large consulting firms, plus an assortment of names that aren't as familiar...most likely smaller, local consulting firms like your own.

As the representative from Simex begins to describe the requirements for the contract, he passes out a statement of work and evaluation criteria (see pages 77 to 79). As he proceeds, most members of the audience try to determine the answers to the same initial question: What is the main or real problem that most likely is not obvious to the client?

Secondary questions, also important, include: How many labor-hours will this project take and at what level of expertise? Can we staff the project alone or will we have to bring in additional help? Is this a job we can deliver on? Is is a job we want? What is the potential for profit on this contract? What is our firm's chance of being selected? How should we best sell our abilities? Who should work on the proposal?

REQUEST FOR PROPOSAL

I. Statement of Work

A. Scope

The Simex Corporation is seeking qualified assistance to evaluate and recommend changes in areas including, but not limited to, its strategic plan, marketing efforts, and organizational effectiveness.

B. Background

In the last few years, the Simex Corporation has experienced a decrease in market share due in part to increased numbers and types of competitors and in part to dynamic shifts in market needs and expectations. Simex has decided to seek outside expertise to help redefine its role in the marketplace and recommend appropriate changes to effectively meet that role.

C. Qualifications of Consultant

Consultant assigned to this task must be experienced in performing analysis and evaluation of internal, market, and competitive data. This should include an appropriate number of individuals from each of the following categories:

1. *Management personnel* The supervising partner on this project shall have a master's degree in a related field and ten to twelve years of directly applicable experience in marketing, organizational design, and strategic planning, at least three of which are with the bidding contractor.
2. *Senior consultants* The senior consultant responsible for coordination, analysis, scheduling, etc. needed for this project shall have a master's degree in a related field and five to seven years of directly related experience.
3. *Associate consultants* Associate consultants working on this project shall have a bachelor's degree and two to three years of related experience.

4. *Technicians / statisticians* The contractor is responsible for obtaining specialized assistance, as in technicians and statisticians, as needed for the input and analysis of data related to the project.

D. Facilities Requirements

The consultant will have access to necessary computing facilities for the organization, evaluation, and demonstration of data and resulting recommendations. These capabilities should include adequate modeling and forecasting activities as necessary for proper analysis.

E. Travel Requirements

The contractor shall be allowed travel expenses to primary facilities at Simex for key project members up to 12 percent of the contracted fees. Travel will also be reimbursed for client interviews as deemed necessary and reasonable. It is estimated that total trip days should not exceed thirteen.

F. Payment Basis

Contract bids will be accepted on an hours-worked basis, payable at regular intervals over the life of the contract. Changes or additions to the basic contract shall be made upon written confirmation by the contractor and Simex. Payment rate and number of hours approved to be adjusted if the contracted scope of the project changes as confirmed by written notice of both parties.

II. Evaluation Criteria

All bids will be judged according to the following criteria, listed here in greatest to least importance.

A. Cost

B. Problem Expertise

1. *Previous experience* Professional approach and understanding of problems of a related nature, as evidenced by successfully completed previous contracts, related background, and so on.

2. *Technical know-how* In the collection and analysis of necessary data, including utilization of computer capabilities of modeling and forecasting.

C. Personnel Requirements
Knowledge, experience, and qualifications as reflected in the resumés of proposed personnel in the order as stated in the statement of work.

D. Management / Company Orientation
Management capabilities and company orientation toward successful completion of projects of this nature. Some emphasis on the continuity and stability of contractor workforce.

The company's representative adds some details to the written Request For Proposal and then takes questions from the group. The closing questions become very direct...

CONSULTANT A: How accessible will personnel and information be to the consultant?

SPOKESPERSON: This project has the complete endorsement of our top management and they have indicated a willingness to have necessary records or personnel at the full disposal of the consulting organization.

CONSULTANT B: What is the timing on this project and your decision to select a consultant?

SPOKESPERSON: We want to move ahead as quickly as possible and hope to make a decision within ten days of the proposal submission deadline. This stage of the work should then be completed within three to four months.

CONSULTANT C: You just said "this stage." Do you see this as a feasibility study for a larger contract or as a one-time need?

SPOKESPERSON: (laughing) All I can say is we've allocated funds for this study which management feels is a pressing need. What happens beyond that is speculation at this point and will in part be dependent upon the recommendations of the firm we hire.

CONSULTANT D: Beyond the requirements you have reviewed, is there a preference for background, expertise, or availability of resources in the firm you are looking to hire?

SPOKESPERSON: If you are asking if this contract is specifically wired for someone, all I can say is that we're looking for a firm that can do the job we've outlined at a fair price.

CONSULTANT E: Is it fair to assume, then, that the project will go to the low bidder, given all other requirements are met?

SPOKESPERSON: Price will be a variable in our decision as weighted in our evaluation criteria.

It becomes obvious that the spokesperson doesn't want to elaborate much on his prepared statement, and the questions quickly drop off. You return to your office and consider what action you should take. You examine your firm's bid sheet criteria, shown opposite.

REGALA STAR CONSULTING COMPANY

Bid Sheet Checklist

1. Does Regala Star have the expertise to bid on this project?
2. Is it an area we are interested in working in?
3. Is it a company we are interested in working for?
4. Have we done similar work for other firms?
5. Have we done similar work for this firm?
6. Do we have tools or resources that give us an edge on doing this work?
7. Are appropriate personnel available for the project?
8. Who is our competition for this work?
9. How do we compare to our competition in the following areas:

Cost	Reputation
Schedule	Contacts
Expertise	Other

10. Will a bid on this project detract from other commitments that we have?
11. Is there significant profit potential on the project?
12. Can this project lead to additional work within the firm or in other firms?
13. Is the cost of bidding reasonable?

Your firm has done related jobs in the industry, but never for this corporation. Your staffing is tight right now, but that has never stopped you from taking on new work in the past. You can always hire additional help as necessary. At the very least, you feel it would not be a problem to obtain letters of intent from potential employees who will come on board if the contract is won. There is also the option of "baiting" the proposal with your best people and later substituting others after the contract is awarded.

A formal proposal on this project will take some time and effort on the part of your firm. In some ways, you have to solve Simex's problems prior to effectively bidding on this contract in order to intelligently estimate the type and amount of work that will be required and the cost of that work. Although you've done similar work before, the estimating and development of a detailed proposal can be an expensive task in itself. If you think your chances of getting this contract are small, you don't want to waste time and resources bidding on the project.

A rough estimate of the work required, however, won't be too time-consuming. You can do a quick cost estimate for the project by estimating the direct-labor expenses (that is, the approximate number of labor-hours needed in each personnel category, and the cost per hour of employees in those categories), multiplying this figure by your overhead rate, and adding direct expenses.

This will enable you to come up with an intitial "best guess" as to Regala Star's cost for doing the project. Fortunately, your firm keeps its overhead as low as possible by charging most employee hours—including management and administrative personnel—directly to contracts. You thus have an advantage in being able to make low, competitive bids.

You don't have a lot of flexibility in who you will bid—you are pretty much limited to who is qualified and available. Where you do have flexibility is in your estimate of the number of projected hours you anticipate the project will take. Your hour estimate is, in fact, the key cost variable in the bid. You can choose to be realistic, aggressive (low), or cautious (high) in your hour estimate. Once you have decided on the number of hours, you simple multiply that number by your billing rate and add your anticipated direct expenses.

The lower the hourly rates you charge the better chance you have of getting the contract (all other things being equal). Of course, the individuals doing the work have to be qualified, and the more qualified they are, the higher their billing rates. You could staff the project at minimum qualifications, but in so doing, you run the risk of producing lower-quality work—or even botching the job. Bringing in high-priced expertise to save a problem project, although rarely done, will often times wipe out any profit that might have been realized on that job.

Your initial labor estimates for this project are for two to three people for a month or so, plus typical support staff. This might place your costs at \$40,000 to 60,000 (small for your firm), depending again upon the number of hours you estimate the project will take and who exactly you use to do the work.

One of the big unknowns, however, is the prospect of doing additional work at Simex—either as a follow-up to this project, or because you will have established a working relationship with a new, sizable client. For example, although this is a relatively small contract, it could quite naturally lead to the installation of a major computing and information system. If Regala Star does the front work, your firm will have an inside track on obtaining a substantially larger contract.

Your competition is stiff for this contract, which means that if you really want this job, you'll have to bid aggressively for it. You might even be tempted to take a loss on the project if you think it has the chance of leading to more significant work. Then again, you don't make money by giving your time away. You can make a fair guess as to what the major competitors will bid based upon your previous experience with them in the marketplace. Several competing firms are likely to price their work at a premium for this contract, especially since it is a relatively small project. Other competing firms will bid low in an attempt to undercut their competition. If such a low bidder were to win the contract, the firm would either expect a planned write-off (loss) for breaking in with a new company, or it would would attempt to increase the number of approved hours as the project progressed.

At this point, you contemplate your bid options and decide on a bidding strategy in relation to your initial cost estimates.

YOUR CHOICE

1A Bid the contract using a high labor-hour estimate. See below.

1B Bid the contract using a realistic labor-hour estimate. See page 84.

1C Bid the contract using a low labor-hour estimate. See page 84.

1D Bid the contract at cost, with a planned write-off. See page 85.

1A **Bid the contract using a high labor-hour estimate.**

Your proposal is not accepted. Although your firm had a respectable burden rate, the contract was still price-sensitive enough to require you to trim your profit to stay in the running. Fortunately, the deadline for bids has not passed and the company will allow you to modify your initial proposal.

−3 Points; Choose Again:

1B Bid the contract using a realistic labor-rate estimate. See page 84.

1C Bid the contract using a low labor-hour estimate. See page 84.

1D Bid the contract at cost, with a planned write-off. See page 85.

1B Bid the contract using a realistic labor-hour estimate.

Simex asks for a "best and final" offer from you. In addition, they want to know why you used two senior consultants rather than one, and if you can cut your travel budget by a third.

You make changes on both items, and then decide if you should vary your labor-hour estimate as well.

+2 Points; Choose Again:

1D Rebid the contract at cost, with a planned write-off. See page 85.

1E Rebid the contract using the same labor-hour estimate. See page 85.

1C Bid the contract using a low labor-hour estimate.

Simex asks for "clarification" of your bid. Specifically, they want to know if you plan to include someone on the project who has specific "turnaround" experience. That is, someone who has taken over a declining operation and made it profitable.

Upon reflection, you decide that such an individual would be invaluable on this particular project. You locate a résumé to include in your revised proposal and decide if you should vary your cost bid, as well.

+2 Points; Choose Again:

1B Rebid the contract using a realistic labor-hour estimate. See page 84.

1D Rebid the contract at cost, with a planned write-off. See page 85.

1E Rebid the contract using the same labor-hour estimate. See page 85.

1F Rebid the contract at below cost, to increase your chances winning the bid. See page 85.

1D **Bid the contract at cost, with a planned write-off.**

Your bid is accepted! You won't make any money on this job, but you've acquired a new client with potential for additional work.

−2 Points; Go to Decision #2, page 86.

1E **Rebid the contract using the same labor-hour estimate.**

Your bid is accepted! In addition, the contract looks as though it will be quite profitable for your firm.

+3 Points; Go to Decision #2, page 86.

1F **Rebid the contract at below cost, increasing your chances of winning the bid.**

Your bid is accepted! Unfortunately, you are going to lose money on the work, but at least you're in the door!

−2 Points; Go to Decision #2, page 86.

DECISION #2: PROJECT STAFFING

You won the bid, and after a brief celebration you start to conceptualize the specific design for the project. Your top concern is staffing. The bid allows for a range of personnel within agreed-upon categories of expertise. Now you must fill in names and schedules, coordinating the project with current workloads and availability. You start by selecting the project manager. This would be a good project for either Sally Murphy or Bud Jones to lead.

Sally Murphy is a consultant who has been with the firm for three years and has worked on several major consulting assignments. Sally, in addition, did much of the preliminary work for the proposal, and should be ready for an increase in responsibility. (See Sally's résumé for additional details.)

Bud Jones has been a project leader a half-dozen times over the last two years. He worked for a competitor of Simex for two years and would be good for this project given his length and type of experience. In fact, he would have been more involved in developing the proposal if the timing had not conflicted with several other projects he was managing. (See Bud's résumé for additional details.)

RÉSUMÉ OF SALLY MURPHY

Experience

Research Associate REGALA STAR CONSULTING 1984 to present

Extensive project support and information collection for several new and existing clients. Merit increase for outstanding effort.

Marketing Trainee McKESSON DISTRIBUTION 1979–82

Rotated responsibilities throughout several marketing positions. Typical responsibilities included demographics analysis, customer interface, and part of a new product introduction team.

Education

Masters in Business Administration, Stanford University, May 1984.
Emphasis in marketing and finance.
BA in Political Science, College of William and Mary, June 1979.

Additional Information

Bright, dependable, hardworking. Fluent in French. Willing to travel, will relocate if necessary.

RÉSUMÉ OF BUD JONES

Experience

Project Manager REGALA STAR CONSULTING 1984 to Present

Numerous assignments, which have included complete coordination and client interface, budgeting, billing, and related responsibilities. Initially joined Regala Star as a Senior Consultant in 1979.

Production Manager MEXA CORPORATION 1974 to 1978

All aspects of coordination of production line, including supervision of 37 people, equipment maintenance, resource allocation, and so forth.

Production Supervisor BENLUX INDUSTRIAL 1972 to 1974

Supervised 12 individuals in final assembly. Responsible for scheduling, management interface, and equipment repair.

Education

Masters in Business Administration, University of Missouri, June 1970.
Emphasis in production control.
BS in Engineering, Ohio State University, June 1967.

Additional Information

Good management and coordination skills. Reliable. Especially skilled at troubleshooting and customer relations.

You obtained the contract primarily because of a relatively low bid, so it would make the most sense to use junior staff as much as possible, since they bill out at a lower rate. If you select Sally, you will be likely to obtain a respectable profit on this contract. In this regard, Sally is the more logical choice, although you will probably have to oversee the work a little more than usual since she doesn't have a lot of experience. On the other hand, you want to be sure you have someone in charge who you can count on to produce quality work and satisfy the client—and you know Bud will deliver. Using someone of Bud's caliber will be expensive, however, and his high cost will diminish the overall profitability of the project. Plus, Bud already has a heavy workload.

You reflect upon the relative merits and potential liabilities that each individual brings to the project, once again review their résumés, and then choose between them.

YOUR CHOICE

2A You select Sally to lead the project. See below.

2B You select Bud to lead the project. See below.

2A You select Sally to lead the project.

Sally is elated!

+2 Points; Go to Decision #3, page 90.

2B You select Bud to lead the project.

Unfortunately, it turns out that Bud already has too heavy a workload to take on a new project. He declines the offer.

0 Points; Default to Choice 2C, page 90.

2C You select Sally to lead the project.

Sally is pleased, but definitely not as excited since she knows she was your second choice. She has lost some trust in you, and you have appeared to be indecisive and inconsistent.

−1 Point; Go to Decision #3, below.

DECISION #3: CLIENT HOSTILITY

"I've never been so insulted in my life!" Sally says, barging into your office unannounced and seemingly oblivious to the fact that you are on the phone. You cut your conversation short, and turn to speak with her as she paces in front of your desk.

YOU: What's the problem, Sally?

SALLY: I just came from a meeting with Gus Fenhart—if you can call it a meeting. He's vice-president of marketing for Simex and I thought he would be a good person to start with on sorting out some of the problems they're having. What a mistake!

YOU: He wasn't helpful, I take it.

SALLY: Helpful! He would barely talk to me. He questioned my experience and credentials. He practically accused me of trying to place the blame for Simex's problems on him and his department. He gave me a lecture about marketing conditions and another one about consultants. He went so far as to suggest the only reason he met with me was because of an edict the CEO sent out.

YOU: Sounds like a lot of animosity on his part. How did you handle it?

SALLY: How could I handle it? I listened, tried to explain the scope of our task, and tried to ask questions about his department—all with little success. I finally decided to just write off the meeting and leave before I lost my cool—he was really starting to get to me.

YOU: What are you going to do about it now?

SALLY: Well, I can't force him to be cooperative. I guess I can try to work around him—you know—collect information from his subordinates and colleagues. That's always awkward though. Why don't you call the CEO and have him talk to this guy?

YOU: I could do that if you feel it's necessary, but it sure isn't going to help your credibility much.

SALLY: Yeah, you're probably right. Well I'm at a loss as to what to do. I can go on with some other interviews, or work on the survey data, but the marketing department seems pretty central to this problem. What do you think?

YOU: Why don't we both think it over and talk again tomorrow.

After Sally leaves, you think about the situation. You are as concerned about her reaction to the client as you were about the client's open hostility, which tends to be a common problem in consulting. Perhaps she isn't quite ready for this assignment. Until now, Sally has primarily been supporting other consultants, and has not served as a project leader. You have no doubt about her analytical abilities, but her interpersonal skills might still need refining.

It is early enough in the project to assign a more experienced person to the task, but that will likely upset Sally, and could possibly blemish her career at Regala Star. There would be certain ramifications with the uncooperative client as well. A replacement might make him think he "won" the confrontation and only encourage him to be more uncooperative with another consultant.

Or perhaps you are jumping to conclusions. You do, after all, feel that Sally has the potential to do the job. Maybe she can effectively handle the situation if given the proper guidance. You could tell her how you'd handle such an uncooperative client or have her speak with others at your firm about feasible approaches. You could role-play her next meeting with the client. Perhaps you could even accompany her the next time she meets with the client and serve as an intermediary.

Whatever you decide to do, you know that ultimate responsibility for the success of the project lies solely with you. If there are complications which are likely to become larger problems, it would be best to clear them up while they are still manageable. You reflect on the possibilities and decide on your course of action:

YOUR CHOICE

3A Replace Sally with a more experienced consultant. See page 92.

3B Have Sally get the information she needs from others. See page 92.

3C Plan to accompany Sally to her next meeting with the client. See page 93.

3D Have Sally meet again with the client on her own to try to work things out. See page 94.

3E Ask the CEO to tell his vice-president of marketing to cooperate. See page 94.

3A Replace Sally with a more experienced consultant.

Sally confronts you in front of others at the firm. She claims you should give her more support, not less, and threatens to quit the firm. Your managerial skill is brought into question. The matter promises to get worse before it gets better...

−2 Points; Choose Again:

3F Reinstate Sally on the project. See page 95.

3G Let Sally quit the firm. See page 95.

3B Have Sally get the information she needs from others.

This is an okay interim solution, but Sally is quite likely going to need to deal with the hostile client again, and the sooner she smooths over the problems in their relationship the better.

0 Points; Choose Again:

3D Have Sally meet again with the client on her own to try to work things out. See page 94.

3E Ask the CEO to tell his vice-president of marketing to cooperate. See page 94.

3F Let Sally handle the problem as she sees fit. See page 95.

3C **Plan to accompany Sally to her next meeting with the client.**

This is the preferred solution. You can't risk sending Sally alone since she was upset by the vice-president of marketing's hostility and might not be able to deal with the situation successfully. He needs reassurance and he needs to be managed, and Sally hasn't displayed the skills necessary to manage him. You run the risk of having it look like you are intervening to rescue her, but you can probably minimize that appearance by openly supporting her in your meeting. You might also send another more senior person with her to deal with the vice-president, while Sally deals with lower level people.

+4 Points; Please Continue...

Unfortunately, the client is equally hostile to you. Now he's your problem as well as Sally's. You choose to:

3B Have Sally get the information she needs from others. See page 92.

3E Ask the CEO to tell his vice-president of marketing to cooperate. See page 94.

3I Keep talking with the client until you convince him that you are there to help him. See page 96.

3D Have Sally meet again with the client on her own to try to work things out.

A good decision! Effective consulting requires a high degree of interpersonal skills, and if Sally is lacking in that area she needs to work on it sooner, not later. You run some risk that the problem may grow worse, and the client might feel that Sally is forcing him to accept her. You still, however, have plenty of time to make additional corrections if they are necessary and you will be saving your trump card—intervention by a more senior consultant (yourself or someone else) for a time when it is truly necessary.

+3 Points; Please Continue...

Predictably, the client is not easily won over. Sally returns to you with a negative report and again seeks your advice.

YOUR CHOICE

3C Plan to accompany Sally to her next meeting with the client. See page 93.

3E Ask the CEO to tell his vice-president of marketing to cooperate. See page 94.

3J Have Sally get the information she needs from others. See page 96.

3K You decide to do nothing. See page 96.

3E Ask the CEO to tell his vice-president of marketing to cooperate.

A strong-armed solution, not likely to win you many points with the hostile client, especially so early in your relationship. Sally gets the information she needs but she and the firm lose goodwill in the process.

−3 Points; Go to Decision #4, page 97.

3F Reinstate Sally on the project.

You decide that perhaps you acted too hastily in pulling Sally off the project. You have to swallow your pride, but a good manager isn't afraid to say he made a mistake.

+1 Points; Choose Again:

3B Have Sally get the information she needs from others. See page 92.

3C Plan to accompany Sally to her next meeting with the client. See page 93.

3D Have Sally meet again with the client on her own to try to work things out. See page 94.

3E Ask the CEO to tell his vice-president of marketing to cooperate. See page 94.

3G Let Sally quit the firm.

The senior partner of Regala Star Consulting comes to talk with you about the situation and asks you to hire her back.

−3 Points; Choose Again:

3B Have Sally get the information she needs from others. See page 92.

3C Plan to accompany Sally to her next meeting with the client. See page 93.

3D Have Sally meet again with the client on her own to try to work things out. See page 94.

3E Ask the CEO to tell his vice-president of marketing to cooperate. See page 94.

3H Let Sally handle the problem as she sees fit.

Not a bad selection, especially if you trust her judgment and want her problems to remain her problems. Of course, she could really blow it and lose a major client for you too! Consulting is a "people business" and it is important for you to show trust in your own people.

+2 Points; Go to Decision #4, page 97.

3I Keep talking to the client until you convince him that you are there to help him.

Not an easy choice to make, but a sound decision. You may not succeed in winning the client over, but it is important to invest the time trying—especially since it is early in the contract.

+4 Points; Go to Decision #4, page 97.

3J Have Sally get the information she needs from others.

At this juncture, it is best for the project to move on and not become completely snarled by one uncooperative person.

+2 Points; Go to Decision #4, page 97.

3K You decide to do nothing.

No sense in overreacting! You have a lot of confidence in Sally and she eventually is able to win the client over.

+2 Points; Go to Decision #4, page 97.

DECISION #4: CLIENT INVOLVEMENT

After estimating the amount and types of data that will be needed, you and Sally finalize a design for the project. The remaining team assignments are made based upon availability and expertise of personnel. The final selection has primarily been made from existing staff members, but it also includes a recent hire. The workload and specific timing is then calculated for various stages of the project to meet the deliverables that were established in the contract.

"Well, that takes care of the main details," you say, getting up to get some more coffee. "Of course, it's all contingent upon the client's approval, but I'm confident they'll readily agree with our staffing recommendations. The one factor we really haven't discussed, however, is the amount of client involvement we want on our project team. Do you have a feeling about that, Sally?"

"This seems to be a sensitive problem at Simex," Sally observes. "Already rumors are being spread that the end result will include some terminations. The amount of client involvement on our project team will have a significant impact on this job. On the one hand, it makes sense to keep the client informed along the way, although that might feed the rumor mill. On the other hand, it might make more sense to let the client know our recommendations after all our research and interviews are completed so as to be more objective in our analysis."

Sally is raising some good points about client involvement. The client can and does provide a great deal of manpower and timely information during a project. But they can get in the way as well. If clients are too closely involved during the process it becomes difficult not to shape recommendations around their preferences. When this happens, you do the client a disservice by telling them what they want to hear, not necessarily what they need to hear, which is most likely what they hired you for.

On this particular project you should consider who is most likely to want to help you in the client organization as well as who is likely to try to stand in your way. Initially, you know that top management of the client organization is clearly on your side, an asset you will try not to rely upon unless absolutely necessary. You are not entirely sure who might be against you, although you have already had a run in with members of the marketing department, especially the vice-president.

It is also important to determine who is most likely to be affected by the final recommendations that are offered—you are likely to want to gain the support of those individuals from the very start. In this case it is quite likely that those people who will be most affected by your recommendations are the same as those who are initially threatened by your presence and thus unsupportive of your activities.

You weigh these considerations and Sally's comments and then decide how much representation you want the client to have during the project. Specifically, how many individuals from the client organization do you want on the project team?

YOUR CHOICE

4A None—so as to keep results of the team as unbiased as possible. See page 98.

4B One—so as to have the client's views represented in person. See page 99.

4C Several—so as to have a range of client views represented. See page 99.

4D Many—so as to involve the client as much as posible as the project proceeds. See page 100.

4A None—so as to keep results of the team as unbiased as possible.

Not a good decision. You're doing the work for the client organization, and you can't afford to surprise them with your results. You need to closely work with the client organization during all aspects of the project to give them ownership in the work, progress, and final recommendations. Otherwise, it may be difficult to sell your final recommendations and satisfy the client's expectations.

−3 Points; Please Choose Again:

4B One—so as to have the client's views represented in person. See below.

4C Several—so as to have a range of client views represented. See below.

4D Many—so as to involve the client as much as possible at the project proceeds. See page 100.

4B One—so as to have the client's views represented in person.

Good choice.

+2 Points; Please Continue...

Who would you specifically like as the client representative?

YOUR CHOICE

4E The CEO of Simex. See page 101.

4F The vice-president of production at Simex. See page 101.

4G The vice-president of marketing at Simex. See page 102.

4H The vice-president of engineering at Simex. See page 102.

4I The vice-president of human resources at Simex. See page 102.

4C Several—so as to have a range of client views represented.

Wise choice! Not only do you want the client's views represented, more importantly, you want the client involved in the process so that they will develop ownership for whatever recommendations you finally make and feel pleased with the job your firm did.

+3 Points; Please Continue...

Who from the client organization would you most like to have on the project team?

YOUR CHOICE

4E The CEO of Simex. See page 101.

4F The vice-president of production at Simex. See page 101.

4G The vice-president of marketing at Simex. See page 102.

4H The vice-president of engineering at Simex. See page 102.

4I The vice-president of human resources at Simex. See page 102.

4D **Many—so as to involve the client as much as possible as the project proceeds.**

Good. It makes sense to involve the client as much as possible and in the process gain their implied and implicit acceptance of the work you are doing.

+1 Points; Please Continue...

It may seem like a trivial matter, but does it matter to you if there are a greater or fewer number of clients represented on the project team than from your consulting organization?

YOUR CHOICE

4J Yes—preferably there should be a relatively greater number of client representatives. See page 102.

4K Yes—preferably there should be a relatively fewer number of client representatives. See page 103.

4L No—the balance of client-to-consultant representatives on the project makes no difference to me. See page 104.

4E The CEO of Simex.

The CEO is too busy to be a part of another "task force." He assigns an aide to represent him and to keep him informed of progress on the project. You would have preferred someone in line management but you don't want to veto the CEO's choice.

−1 Point; Please Continue...

You decide that you definitely need to have someone from line management represented on the project team. Who would you prefer?

YOUR CHOICE

4F The vice-president of production at Simex. See below.

4G The vice-president of marketing at Simex. See page 102.

4H The vice-president of engineering at Simex. See page 102.
(Do not choose if previously selected.)

4F The vice-president of engineering at Simex.

The vice-president of engineering declines your invitation, and is a bit puzzled why his specific involvement was so important to you.

0 Points; Choose Again:

4E The CEO of Simex. See above.

4G The vice-president of marketing at Simex. See page 102.

4H The vice-president of engineering at Simex. See page 102.

4I The vice-president of human resources at Simex. See page 102.

4G The vice-president of marketing at Simex.

An excellent choice, since the project most directly affects marketing, but especially since this individual initially seems hostile to your efforts. Having him officially involved as part of the project team will give you adequate time to co-opt his support.

+3 Points; Go to Decision #5, page 104.

4H The vice-president of production at Simex.

The vice-president of production eagerly accepts your offer to be a part of the project. Unfortunately, he is not in the best position to assist with information or organizational support for your efforts, and his acceptance might be politically motivated.

−2 Points; Go to Decision #5, page 104.

4I The vice-president of human resources at Simex.

Surely you jest! Are you getting an early start on some potential layoffs? Your choice has completely alienated you from line management at Simex.

−5 Points; Go to Decision #5, page 104.

4J Yes—preferably there should be a relatively greater number of client representatives.

You will have lots of involvement, but most likely a lot less control as well.

−2 Points; Please Continue . . .

Of the client representatives, is there one individual who you would especially like to have on the project team?

YOUR CHOICE

4E The CEO of Simex. See page 101.

4F The vice-president of production at Simex. See page 101.

4G The vice-president of marketing at Simex. See page 102.

4H The vice-president of engineering at Simex. See page 102.

4I The vice-president of human resources at Simex. See page 102.

4K **Yes—preferably there should be a relatively fewer number of client representatives.**

Good, that way you have a better chance of maintaining control of the project.

+2 Point; Please Continue...

Of the client representatives, is there one individual who you would especially like to have on the project team?

YOUR CHOICE

4E The CEO of Simex. See page 101.

4F The vice-president of production at Simex. See page 101.

4G The vice-president of marketing at Simex. See page 102.

4H The vice-president of engineering at Simex. See page 102.

4I The vice-president of human resources at Simex. See page 102.

4L No—the balance of client to consultant representatives on the project makes no difference to me.

Well it should make a difference! If you don't care whether or not you have control over the project you are likely to end up without it!

−3 Points; Please Continue...

Of the client representatives, is there one individual who you would especially like to have on the project team?

YOUR CHOICE

4E The CEO of Simex. See page 101.

4F The vice-president of production at Simex. See page 101.

4G The vice-president of marketing at Simex. See page 102.

4H The vice-president of engineering at Simex. See page 102.

4I The vice-president of human resources at Simex. See page 102.

Decision #5: Report of Findings

Sally and her team completed their information gathering and are now preparing their report of findings for the client. Since you will be delivering the recommendations, Sally briefs you on the team's conclusions...

"We've seen the pattern before," Sally says to start her presentation. "Simex is organized for the past and not for the future. What we thought was a marketing problem is actually a much broader and complicated issue. Simex is organized by function, in a way that allows for efficient production. They need to be organized by client and oriented toward the market. They currently produce cutting-edge innovations in their products with little regard as to whether or not the advanced technology is desirable to their client base or if clients are even willing to pay for the innovations."

"A prime example, which is indicative of much more substantial problems, is the recent marketing plan for their latest laser printer. There was very little coordination between departments on that product. For example, many of the product's innovations were technical advances, but of secondary importance to buyers in this market. The marketing department could have easily told engineering that, but they were never asked."

"Marketing didn't communicate well with the production department, either. Adequate inventory of the product did not exist to support the marketing effort in a timely way. Production was stepped up to meet the surge of orders, but by the time the product was delivered, a significant percentage of orders had been cancelled due to the delay."

"If they reorganize around their client base, a major product introduction would be better coordinated. In addition, redundant department functions could be eliminated and their responsiveness to the market greatly increased."

"What are the major obstacles to reorganizing?" you interject.

"There are several. For one, there is a lot of personal attachment to the current organizational structure. For example, the engineering department prides itself on its independence. Their preference is to work on researching and developing cutting-edge technology. In this way they feel more a part of a professional calling than as employees to a company selling products. In fact, they blame sales for most of the company's problems." Their preference is to work on researching and developing cutting-edge technology. In this way they feel more a part of a professional calling than as employees to a company selling products. In fact, they blame sales for most of the company's problems."

"Another problem is the effect such a reorganization would have on top management. If the marketing department is decentralized and assigned to specific clients or products, the marketing infrastructure within the organization is greatly weakened. It thus becomes more difficult to justify the number of vice-presidents which exist in that function. Reassignments and terminations would be imminent and those individuals that did remain would have considerably less clout in the organization."

"The organization has very strong, centrally organized functions which have developed into fiefdoms. Many managers don't have the skills to handle their current jobs, having advanced more through loyalty to management than functional competence. That's not news that is going to be easy for them to take, but they need to hear it."

As the partner in charge of this project, you will be presenting the team's findings to the client. Sally's analysis seems valid, and you consider the best method of relating the recommendations. More than just passing on information, you need to sell your recommendations to the client, in part so that they feel they got their money's worth out of the contract, and in part to ensure your firm's inclusion in the implementation of any recommendations.

At the same time, however, this project doesn't have the profit margin or size to justify an extravagant presentation. You don't want to go overboard with a format which is overly elaborate or lavish because you aren't sure a flashy presentation would impress this particular client.

Besides the format for the recommendations (written, oral, or some combination of both), you are debating how formal to be in delivering your findings. Being informal would take some of the punch and surprise out of your work. For example, speaking to key individuals ahead of time about how their area might be adversely affected might make the presentation of the final recommendations somewhat anti-climatic. On the other hand you can "pre-sell" your recommendations if you think they might otherwise meet with resistance. Advance information would, in addition, be a courtesy in some instances in which individuals who would be negatively affected by your recommendations are informed privately ahead of time.

You consider who best to deliver your recommendations...

YOUR CHOICE

5A Informally discuss the findings with the CEO. See below.

5B Contact those individuals who head areas which will be negatively affected by your report. See page 107.

5C Plan a day-long session with the CEO and his key department heads to go over your recommendations. See page 107.

5D Submit a thorough written report of your findings as per your contract. See page 108.

5A Informally discuss the findings with the CEO.

It's always good to keep the "bigs" informed. Giving the CEO information lets him have the inside track as to what's going on in his firm, which makes for good public relations... and key support.

+2 Points; Choose Again:

5C Plan a day-long session with the CEO and his key department heads to go over your recommendations. See below.

5E Submit a thorough written report of your findings as per your contract. See page 108.

5B Contact those individuals who head areas which will be negatively affected by your report.

This is a nice courtesy, which keeps those that have the most to lose from being blindsided.

+1 Point; Please Continue...

Unfortunately, the regional sales manager doesn't appreciate your consideration and contacts the CEO directly to recommend that the contract be cancelled.

YOUR CHOICE

5E Submit a thorough written report of your findings as per your contract. See page 108.

5F Informally discuss the findings with the CEO. See page 109.

5G Plan a day-long session with the CEO and his key department heads to go over your recommendations. See page 109.

5C Plan a day-long session with the CEO and his key department heads to go over your recommendations.

An excellent means of explaining your findings in a manner which allows for adequate discussion and planning and a high likelihood of commitment to your recommendations. The cost may be higher, but it is money well spent in consulting.

+3 Points; Please Continue...

Is there any other follow-up you would like to make for this contract?

YOUR CHOICE

5E Submit a thorough written report of your findings as per your contract. See below.

5H Schedule a follow-up session for three months from now. See page 109.

5D Submit a thorough written report of your findings as per your contract.

This is not a good first step. You lose the chance to sell your recommendations, so the likelihood that they will be accepted "as is" decreases, as does the possibility of your further involvement with the firm.

−2 Points; Please Continue...

Your report didn't have the splash you hoped it would. In fact, several key individuals at Simex have not even read it yet. You decide to conduct one or more informal meetings. Which one do you most prefer?

YOUR CHOICE

5F Informally discuss the findings with the CEO. See page 109.

5B Contact those individuals who head areas which will be negatively affected by your report. See page 107.

5G Plan a day-long session with the CEO and his key department heads to go over your recommendations. See page 107.

5E Submit a thorough written report of your findings as per your contract.

This is a necessary step to take in your contract, best made after your findings and recommendations have been informally discussed.

+1 Point; Go to Decision #6, page 220.

5F Informally discuss the findings with the CEO.

This choice would be a crucial step to take at this stage of your recommendations, given you had some preliminary negative reactions to your recommendations.

+2 Points; Choose Again:

5C Plan a day-long session with the CEO and his key department heads to go over your recommendations. See page 107.

5E Submit a thorough written report of your findings as per your contract. See page 108.

5G Plan a day-long session with the CEO and his key department heads to go over your recommendations.

A risky decision! Although this choice is usually an effective method of presenting your findings, at this point individual negative reactions may jeopardize the session's effectiveness and the acceptability of your recommendations.

−3 Points; Go to Decision #6, page 110.

5H Schedule a follow-up session for three months from now.

An excellent idea both to see that recommendations are being successfully implemented and to increase your chances of selling some additional services.

+5 Points; Please Go to Decision #6, page 110.

DECISION #6: UNFORESEEN DELAYS

"So what's the current status of the reorganization at Simex?" you ask Sally during your weekly review of projects.

"It's going a bit slower than we had hoped. One reason is we've uncovered some additional needs they have and a second reason is that the client is having doubts about some of our recommendations."

"What additional needs?" you ask.

"Well, we found out that sections of their accounts receivable process were still manual, so as a side project we've been evaluating computer systems for that area."

"What doubts?" you ask.

"We had recommended—and the client agreed—that there were redundancies in the sales coverage. Instead of having a sales staff for each major product, we suggested having the sales department organize around the kinds and sizes of clients to be more responsive to their needs. Now, in some cases one salesperson serves an entire client organization that previously had seven or eight sales representatives calling on it."

"That does seem more efficient; what's the problem?"

"The problem is our client is now thinking that the cutbacks might be too extreme. Their feeling is that the reduced exposure with their clients might lead to reduced business. Of course, I'm sure resistance marketing was a factor as well. It's all adding up to more time than we bargained for, and perhaps more than they're willing to pay. We could still try to cut corners to meet our reorganization deadlines on time if you feel that schedule is crucial to keep—what do you think?"

"The problem in cutting corners or rushing the job is that the quality we promised the client on this project is likely to be lacking. Besides the risk of client dissatisfaction, we have certain liabilities and fiduciary responsibilities. If, at a later date, Simex can show that we gave them poor advice, I'm sure their legal department would have no hesitation about suing our firm. To say the least, that's not good for business."

"That puts us in a bind, then. How should we handle the delays we're facing?"

The additional work clearly needs to be done, however, perhaps it doesn't need to be done right now, or at least not right now by your consulting firm. You reflect on the pros and cons or handling the unforeseen delays and your experience to date with this client, and offer the following plan of action.

YOUR CHOICE

6A Do the additional work; take the additional costs out of your profits. See below.

6B Do the additional work; bill the client for it. See page 112.

6C Do not do the additional work; discuss a new contract for add-on projects with the client. See page 112.

6D Do not do the additional work; make no reference to it to the client. See page 113.

6A Do the additional work; take the additional costs out of your profits.

This decision shows your concern for solving the client's problems. It also shows why you're not making much money.

−3 Points; Please Continue . . .

The additional work you have chosen to do has thrown off your delivery schedule. How do you wish to handle this?

YOUR CHOICE

6E Renegotiate a delivery schedule with the client. See page 113.

6F Work overtime to make the original deadlines. See page 113.

6B Do the additional work; bill the client for it.

The client is outraged that you would bill him for nonspecified work! Your charges are refused and you have lost considerable goodwill in the process.

−2 Points; Please Continue...

The additional work you have chosen to do has thrown off your delivery schedule. How do you wish to handle this?

YOUR CHOICE

6E Renegotiate a delivery schedule with the client. See page 113.

6F Work overtime to make the original deadlines. See page 113.

6C Do not do the additional work; discuss a new contract for add-on projects with the client.

The client is impressed with your thoroughness and gives you verbal confirmation for the add-on work. You immediately prepare a confirming letter. The final delivery date is quickly approaching and you are eager to come to closure with this contract and keep the client satisfied. You need to make a decision concerning whether to do the add-on work right away or wait for official notice from the client.

+4 Points; Please Choose Again:

YOUR CHOICE

6G Do the add-on work in order to promptly return your full efforts to finishing on time. See page 114.

6H Wait to do the add-on work until you have received written confirmation for it from the client. See page 114.

6D **Do not do the additional work; make no reference to it to the client.**

The client finds out that you chose not to tell them about additional problems you have found. You lose significant goodwill since they no longer feel you have their best interests as a primary objective.

–3 Points; Please Continue...

You attempt to redeem yourself regarding the additional work:

YOUR CHOICE

6A Do the additional work; take the additional costs out of your profits. See page 111.

6B Do the additional work; bill the client for it. See page 112.

6C Do not do the additional work; discuss a new contract for add-on projects with the client. See page 112.

6E **Renegotiate a delivery schedule with the client.**

The client is not flexible in changing their original delivery schedule. In fact, they threaten to charge you liquidated damages if the final deliverable is not met on time. You are left with little choice but to work overtime to meet your contractual agreement.

0 Points; Default to Choice 6F, below.

6F **Work overtime to make the original deadlines.**

This contract is really putting you in debt! You'll have to think twice about being such a nice person...

–2 Points; Go to Decision#7, page 114.

6G **Do the add-on work in order to promptly return your full efforts to finishing on time.**

You finish the final deadline on time and the client is pleased with your work! You don't expect any problems about payment for the extra work, although you never did get the written confirmation returned from the client. Hopefully, they will honor their word!

−1 Point; Go to Decision #7, below.

6H **Wait to do the add-on work until you have received written confirmation for it from the client.**

The client is annoyed that you do not trust his word, but respects you for your professionalism. You have also greatly increased your chances of collecting your fees.

+3 Point; Go to Decision #7, below.

Decision #7: Recovering Fees

"'...for estimated expenses not to exceed $50,000.' That's the specific wording of our contract," the vice-president of the accounting division reads out loud in a slow, steady voice.

You can't believe that what has been considered a successful contract is threatening to go sour over billing procedures.

"Were you less than 100 percent pleased with what we did for you?" you ask point blank.

"We're satisfied—we've already told you that. I'm not sure you did exactly what you claimed you would, but you did a good job nonetheless. I'm just concerned at what price the job was done. From the way I see it, we've already paid you in full for your efforts."

"We've already gone over this several times. All items which exceeded the budget were given verbal confirmation by Simex management and a written notice by our accounting department," you reemphasize.

"I think the key to this situation lies in the statement you just made. Isolated 'verbal confirmation' from individuals who were unfamiliar with the overall budget for this job has little merit from a contractual standpoint. What concerns me is that the piece-meal approval process you have participated in has caused us to exceed the maximum allowed for this contract by $8,000. Had we had the facts in front of us at any one place or time, clearly several of the lower priority add-on projects you initiated would not have been approved."

"Now be reasonable. Had we known all the problems that were going to surface on this project at one time, we obviously would have bid it differently."

An uneasy silence fills the room. The controller continues in a deliberate, unyielding manner...

"From where I sit, that looks like one of the risks in your line of business. We can't be expected to cover for your miscalculations."

"But all the additional increases were approved by management at Simex!"

"Some of those managers thought they were simply verifying preapproved payments for work that had been completed. You've said yourself that others provided only oral confirmation—unfortunately without first checking with our department. I'm sorry, but we're going to have to insist on sticking to our contract as it is written."

You thought that by "progress billing," that is, being paid as different phases of your consulting work were completed, you would be able to avoid any payment hassles on this project. It seems, however, that your client is planning to stiff you on the final payment. Sure, you have a contract, but you would much rather settle this matter out of court to save both goodwill and legal expenses. If you don't recover the remaining portion of the hours billed, the firm will lose money on this contract—which won't make you look too good.

Your primary expense in consulting is your time and that of your staff. In this case, the time has already been spent on this project.

There really isn't any part of the work that can be withheld pending final payment. You can stick by the approvals made by the client's management along the way, even suing if necessary, but that will be at the cost of considerable goodwill. Your chances of doing additional work with the firm in the future will be unlikely. Then again, do you want to work with a place that doesn't honor its debts?? You mull over possible approaches and select a course of action.

YOUR CHOICE

7A Don't pursue the matter; write the loss off to experience. See below.

7B Request payment only on deviations that were approved in writing. See page 117.

7C Identify delays or inefficiencies caused by the client and bill them for those items. See page 117.

7D Go speak to the CEO about the delinquent payment. See page 118.

7E Threaten to sue for the amount owed. Have your legal department write their legal department. See page 118.

7A Don't pursue the matter; write the loss off to experience.

You should at least try to collect, after all you put in quite a few hours beyond your contractual commitment.

−2 Points; Please Choose Again:

YOUR CHOICE

7B Request payment only on deviations that were approved in writing. See page 117.

7C Identify delays or inefficiencies caused by the client and bill them for those items. See page 117.

7D Go speak to the CEO about the deliquent payment. See page 118.

7E Threaten to sue for the amount owed. Have your legal department write their legal department. See page 118.

7F Give a credit towards future work for part of the costs incurred, but insist on full payment now for what is owed. See page 119.

7B **Request payment only on deviations that were approved in writing.**

A nice compromise—the client accepts your offer!

+2 Points; Please Continue...

Did you obtain written confirmation for all add-on work you had done? (Specifically, did you select Choice 6H if given the chance to do so in the last decision point.)

Choose accordingly:

YES Congratulations, you will receive full payment for your work.

+3 Points; Go to Case Analysis, page 121.

OR

NO You might make a note to do this next time. It will make it easier to pay your bills if that's of importance to you.

−3 Points; Go to Case Analysis, page 121.

7C **Identify delays or inefficiencies caused by the client and bill them for those items.**

An excellent way to handle this situation! You still may not get paid, but it appears you are offering a fair compromise with a logical rationale.

+3 Points, Please Continue...

Simex remains hesitant. What do you want to do about this?

YOUR CHOICE

7D Go speak to the CEO about the delinquent payment. See below.

7E Threaten to sue for the amount owed. Have your legal department write their legal department. See below.

7G Do nothing more at this time. See page 120.

7D Go speak to the CEO about the delinquent payment.

If you must, you must. If you do it tactfully, you might be able to salvage the situation. At least you are persistent. The CEO speaks with you briefly concerning the matter and hints that your firm is being petty and shortsighted.

+1 Point; Choose Again:

YOUR CHOICE

7B Request payment only on deviations that were approved in writing. See page 117.

7E Threaten to sue for the amount owed. Have your legal department write their legal department. See below.

7H Give a credit towards future work for part of the costs incurred, but insist on full payment now for what is owed. See page 120.

7E Threaten to sue for the amount owed. Have your legal department write their legal department.

You're not especially interested in working for this firm again, are you? If you do get your money—which is unlikely—it will be in the distant future after extensive legal fees are deducted. It probably wasn't worth the trouble.

−3 Points; Please Continue . . .

Did you obtain written confirmation for all add-on work you had done? (Specifically, did you select Choice 6H if given the chance to do so in Decision #6.)

Choose accordingly:

YES Congratulations, you will receive full payment for your work.

+3 Points; Go to Case Analysis, page 121.

OR

NO You might make a note to do this next time. It will make it easier to pay your bills in the future.

−3 Points; Go to Case Analysis, page 121.

7F **Give a credit towards future work for part of the costs incurred, but insist on full payment now for what is owed.**

A nice compromise, too bad the client didn't go for it. They continue to hold their ground.

0 Points; Choose Again:

7B Request payment only on deviations that were approved in writing. See page 117.

7D Go speak to the CEO about the delinquent payment. See page 118.

7E Threaten to sue for the amount owed. Have your legal department write their legal department. See page 118.

7G Do nothing more at this time. See page 120.

7G **Do nothing more at this time.**

Wise decision! If you had persisted much further, you would have definitely alienated the client. They eventually did decide to pay for their errors and delays—the bulk of the additional costs.

+3 Points, Go to Case Analysis, page 121.

7H **Give a credit towards future work for part of the costs incurred, but insist on full payment now for what is owed.**

The client agrees to your compromise! You get your money, maintain goodwill, plus guarantee future work with the firm.

+2 Points; Go to Case Analysis, page 121.

Results of Consulting Contract: Case Analysis

To see if the contract was profitable, led to additional business for your firm, and/or included personal recognition for you, total the number of points you scored from all your decisions and turn to the page indicated.

+31 points and above. See R1, below.

+24 to +30 points. See R2, page 122.

+17 to +23 points. See R3, page 122.

+10 to +16 points. See R4, page 122.

+4 to +9 points. See R5, page 122.

−3 to +3 points. See R6, page 123.

−4 to −9 points. See R7, page 123.

−10 to −16 points. See R8, page 123.

−17 to −23 points. See R9, page 123.

−24 to −30 points. See R10, page 124.

−31 points and below. See R11, page 124.

R1: Contract is Extremely Profitable
(+31 points or more.)

Your company receives a $1.5 million follow-up contract; you are made partner!

For additional insight into which decisions made an impact on your success, see:

"Decision Analysis," page 125, and then

"Probable Reasons for a Profitable Contract," page 128.

R2: CONTRACT IS PROFITABLE (+24 to +30 points.)

Your company receives an add-on contract; you are given a bonus.

For additional insight into which decisions made an impact on your success, see:

"Decision Analysis," page 125, and then

"Probable Reasons for a Profitable Contract," page 128.

R3: CONTRACT IS PROFITABLE (+17 to +23 points.)

Your company receives a referral; you receive a letter of commendation.

For additional insight into which decisions made an impact on your success, see:

"Decision Analysis," page 125, and then

"Probable Reasons for a Profitable Contract," page 128.

R4: CONTRACT IS PROFITABLE (+10 to +16 points.)

Your company doesn't receive any additional business, but you are given a larger project to manage.

For additional insight into which decisions made an impact on your success, see:

"Decision Analysis," page 125, and then

"Probable Reasons for a Profitable Contract," page 128.

R5: CONTRACT BREAKS EVEN (+4 to +9 points.)

Your company receives add-on work.

For additional insight into which decisions made an impact on your success, see:

"Decision Analysis," page 125, and then

"Contributing Reasons for Breaking Even," page 130.

R6: CONTRACT BREAKS EVEN (−3 to +3 points.)

Your company receives a referral for additional business.

For additional insight into which decisions made an impact on your success, see:

"Decision Analysis," page 125, and then

"Contributing Reasons for Breaking Even," page 130.

R7: CONTRACT BREAKS EVEN (−4 to −9 points.)

No additional work is done for the client.

For additional insight into which decisions made an impact on your success, see:

"Decision Analysis," page 125, and then

"Contributing Reasons for Breaking Even," page 130.

R8: CONTRACT LOSES MONEY (−10 to −16 points.)

Some add-on work is scheduled, but you are criticized at your next performance review.

For additional insight into which decisions made an impact on your success, see:

"Decision Analysis," page 125, and then

"Probable Reasons for an Unprofitable Contract," page 132.

R9: CONTRACT LOSES MONEY (−17 to −23 points.)

Your company manages to obtain a referral from the client; you receive no bonus at the end of the year.

For additional insight into which decisions made an impact on your success, see:

"Decision Analysis," page 125, and then

"Probable Reasons for an Unprofitable Contract," page 132.

R10: Contract Loses Money (−24 to −30 points.)

No additional work is lined up and you get a below average raise at your next review.

For additional insight into which decisions made an impact on your success, see:

"Decision Analysis," page 125, and then

"Probable Reasons for an Unprofitable Contract," page 132.

R11: Contract Loses Money (−31 points and below.)

Your company is sued for negligence; you are fired.

For additional insight into which decisions made an impact on your success, see:

"Decision Analysis," page 125, and then

"Probable Reasons for an Unprofitable Contract," page 132.

RESULTS OF CONSULTING CONTRACT: DECISION ANALYSIS

Here is a brief summary of what you had to do (and why) to obtain maximum points for each decision.

DECISION #1: NEW CONTRACT BID

This was probably the most crucial decision of the selection. In consulting, if you are not successful at getting new contracts, you are not likely to survive for long. There is a lot of work involved in acquiring new clients, which requires the consultant to be able to piece together information from random and unrelated sources. This case was perhaps a bit formal for the small size of the contract, but it gave you exposure to the range of steps writing up and finalizing a contract requires. You received maximum points if you tried to be competitive regarding costs (labor-hours) while at the same time refusing to enter into an agreement which would result in a financial loss.

DECISION #2: PROJECT STAFFING

This was a simplified version of a common decision in consulting: how to staff projects. Usually there are more constraints on individual schedules, and personnel with the necessary skills for specific contract tasks may not be readily available. The choice here was whether to go with a less experienced, better-educated staff member or a more experienced (and higher-paid) member of the staff. The selection was forced (as often happens in real life) so that your preference made little difference in the final selection, due to scheduling constraints.

DECISION #3: CLIENT HOSTILITY

Consultants often have to deal with clients who resent their age, training, experience, and/or manner. Since effective interpersonal skills are essential in a successful consultant, this decision tested a truly critical variable. You had to balance a combination of trust for your own staff member with respect for the client and a strong desire to get the work done without alienating either person. You received maximum points if you addressed the problem in a straightforward manner rather than avoiding or working around the problem.

Decision #4: Client Involvement

This decision sought to explore the issues of task ownership and control in the consulting relationship. It was important to have the right people involved on the assignment to the degree that it affected them and their areas of responsibility. At the same time you needed to retain—in subtle ways—ultimate decision-making control over the project so that you had the most power to influence the final outcome.

Decision #5: Report of Findings

This decision was another test of your interpersonal skills and your ability to use the most effective form of communication to achieve your objectives. Emphasis should have been placed on direct, personal (face-to-face), informal communication that allowed an adequate amount of quality time for you to explain things to and persuade the client.

Decision #6: Unforeseen Delays

This is probably one of the most common problems which consultants face. Your ability to handle this situation effectively would clearly make a difference in the amount of work that was needed to complete the contract and the amount of payment you received. To get the maximum number of points, you needed to make it clear that no unauthorized work would be done until that work had been discussed, approved, and confirmed in writing by the client.

Decision #7: Recovering Fees

This is another important skill, and a common problem as well, in the consulting profession. Your previous actions (in the contract and with handling additional work) would have a strong influence upon how successful you were at collecting due monies. To score highly here, you needed to have balanced a fair, persistent approach with respect for your client and a desire to work again with him or her. In addition, your actions needed to be in the right sequence—not too soon, and not too late. Demanding payment too early would have alienated the client and negated subsequent attempts to collect.

Probable Reasons for a Profitable Contract

Three of the decisions in this case most pertained to the profitability of the contract. Other decisions related more to the quality of your consulting, primarily as it pertained to client relations.

Issue / Choice Number	Comments
PROFITABILITY	
1. Bidding	
1A, 1B	You bid the contract as though you expected to make money from the work—a reasonable expectation!
2. Handling Delays	
6C, 6E	You didn't do extra work for free, and most likely the client didn't expect you to anyway!
6H	You waited until you had written confirmation regarding add-on work.
3. Collecting Fees	
7B, 7C	These were both reasonable and realistic approaches for collecting unpaid fees.
4. Miscellaneous	
5H	You don't get work unless you push for it!

CLIENT RELATIONS

3C, 3D, 3I	You kept at the problem of client hostility in a persistant, professional way.
4C, 4D, 4K	You selected the right number of people to involve on the project.
4E, 4G	You selected the right people to involve on the project.
5A, 5F	It was good to closely involve the CEO.
5C, 5G	A day-long session gave proper attention and consideration to your recommendations.
5H	A follow-up session showed concern and increased your chances for more business.
6G	You were prompt about meeting your deliverables.

Please continue to Case #3, page 144.

Probable Reasons for Breaking Even

You were able to break even either by making a lot of indecisive, safe, noncommital choices, or by being wildly inconsistent so that the effects of excellent decisions were cancelled out by the effects of poor decisions. In the former case, check the decisions listed below for neutral selections, which scored neither high nor low points. In the latter case, see "Probable Reasons for a Profitable/Unprofitable Contract," pages, 128 and 132, respectively.

Issue / Choice Number	Comments
2C	Your judgment was questioned and trust was lost when you made this personnel decision.
3A	You were inconsistent and didn't trust your subordinate.
3B	You avoided the real problem.
3F	Your action was inconsistent and made you appear indecisive.
4D	You weren't sensitive in maintaining control of the project.
4F	This was an illogical, almost random personnel selection.
5B	This was a nice thing to do, but probably risky as well.
5E	You were insensitive as to what would be effective.

6G	Your priorities were out of order. You pleased the client, but caused your own company to lose money as a direct result.
7D	Speaking to the CEO was premature and ineffective.
7F	This choice was not realistic.

Please continue to Case #3, page 135.

Probable Reasons for an Unprofitable Contract

Three of the decisions in this case most pertained to the profitability of the contract. Other decisions related more to the quality of your consulting, primarily as it affected client relations.

Issue / Choice Number	Comments
PROFITABILITY	
1. Bidding	
1C, 1D, 1F	You were not aggressive enough in bidding your work.
2. Handling Delays	
6A, 6B	You should not have done unrequested work without prior approval and a commitment to be paid.
6F	Working overtime cut deeply into your profits.
3. Collecting Fees	
7A	You gave up too easily.
7E	You should have backed down sooner.
4. Miscellaneous	
3A	A more experienced consultant was more expensive.

CLIENT RELATIONS

3E	You alienated yourself by forcing someone to cooperate.
4A, 4B	You needed a greater degree of involvement by the client!
4F, 4H, 4I	You involved the wrong people!
4J	You were insensitive to the need to have adequate control of the project.
5D	This was an ineffective means of gaining support for your recommendations!
6B	Your approach was insensitive and ineffective.
6D	You failed to communicate with the client when it was necessary.

Please continue to Case #3, page 135.

CASE #3

New Age Robotics, Inc.

BRIEFING

High-technology manufacturing holds both high risk and high potential for profitability. Product life cycles are short, but if you are in the right place (with the right marketing and price) at the right time, you will experience exponential success. On the down side, your entire market can be wiped out overnight by a new technical innovation or an entry by a large firm into your market niche. Business is complicated by a greater number of unknowns than are found in most businesses, the greatest of which is not knowing what the future will bring—or how soon!

INDUSTRY DESCRIPTION

The robotics industry expects to experience 30 to 35 percent growth through the 1990s. Sales in 1992 were approximately $2.2 billion. This tremendous growth will affect a large number of supporting industries, such as automated manufacturing and inspection, computer-aided manufacturing, instrumentation, industrial controls, integrated circuits, and machine tools, to name a few. Driving forces in the industry include the major trend in retooling industrial America as led by the Big Three car manufacturers, which are turning to high-technology solutions to increase competitiveness and control costs in a labor-intensive industry.

Firm Description

New Age Robotics, Inc. manufactures a variety of rotational control mechanisms, including motor drives, "indexers" (which program the movements of motor drives), stepping and servo motors, and related products used in automated manufacturing processes such as product assembly. The firm, now in its sixth year of operations, has doubled its revenues each year and will gross $5 million in the current fiscal year.

New Age Robotics was founded by Jason "Spark" Clintmoore, a former engineer at General Eclectic. Spark initially conceived of the original product design (a micro-stepping motor control mechanism) during a coffee break and perfected its design during numerous lunch hours spanning a seven-year period. When Spark asked his supervisor what he thought of the idea, he was told to get back to work. Later in the week Spark asked for and was granted permission to market the product himself, which he successfully did ($25,000 in annual revenues) for two years out of his home. Spark then sought and obtained $300,000 in venture capital from The Oxnard Fund (Boston, MA) and received a second round of funding ($750,000) from the Snearox Corporation a year later. Mr. Clintmoore has since been replaced by a professional management team (a condition of the second round financiers), a move which was in line with the firm's strategic objectives. Mr. Clintmoore maintains a 5 percent share of the firm's stock although he no longer has any say in operations.

Product Description

The main products that New Age Robotics assembles and markets are motor drives, which control the rotational movement of motors (that is, speed, direction, starting, and stopping), and indexers, which control the operations of motor drives (that is, programming a series of commands). The latest product the firm has been developing is called an LMCM (Large Motor Control Mechanism) which would operate high-horsepower motors, mainly found in the robotics and related industries.

Reader Role

You have been head of New Age Robotics for the past two years, a challenging and rewarding position which you have enjoyed immensely. Prior to joining the firm you were vice-president of engineering at Integrated Circuits, a semi-conductor manufacturer. You have a PhD in electrical engineering and an MBA from Stanford, with fifteen years of progressively more responsible experience in engineering and manufacturing environments. You own four percent of the net equity of New Age Robotics, which you were able to purchase at a discount when you took your current position. You are optimistic about the future of the firm but have several concerns which you are trying to address as CEO. Perhaps the foremost of your concerns is a need for the firm to develop new and diverse products so as to remain a viable competitor in the robotics market for years to come.

THE DECISIONS

DECISION #1: NEW PRODUCT PRICING STRATEGY

"Here it is!" Dr. Barney Williams, research director is beaming from ear to ear as he walks into the Monday morning staff meeting carrying a black metal box about the size of a shoebox.

"For a quarter of a million dollars I'd thought we'd at least have the thing chrome-plated," Jack Murphy, vice-president of marketing, sarcastically remarks. Dr. Williams ignores him.

You, however, come to Barney's defense: "The packaging is a final touch, Jack, this is just the prototype—and one we've been eagerly waiting for."

Sara O'Neal, vice-president of finance, picks up your lead: "This is exactly the product we need to introduce in the market to meet our unit volume and dollar growth projections. Good work Barney!"

"Well, we're not entirely there yet," Dr. Williams modestly states. "It's true that this prototype has performed well under tests, but we still haven't field marketed it yet."

"And when will that be, Dr. Williams?" Jack snidely asks.

"To tell you the truth, Jack, I was going to ask you that same question," Barney countered. Everyone breaks out laughing.

The festive mood is appropriate for the introduction of New Age Robotics' most recent innovation: a computer-driven Large Motor Control Mechanism (LMCM) capable of programming the movements of high-horsepower motors. The LMCM has the potential to revolutionize the robotics industry. It brings a new level of precision control to an area of the market which has up to now been limited to simple, repetitive tasks. With the LMCM, the utilization of heavy equipment could be expanded five-fold, opening up a new range of possible applications and markets, and increasing the utilization and profitability of such equipment. The problem is determining the best way to market it. New Age Robotics has found in their own limited experience with new products that the world will not beat a path to your door, even if you do have a better mousetrap. As Bob Isuzki, the new products manager was saying:

"We've got to convince the customer to use our product and then thank him for the opportunity of saving him money while allowing him to make more himself."

"You've got that part right," Jack chimes in. "There is so much change and such a flood of new products in this market that customers are afraid to commit to any specific technology for fear it will be technologically obsolete by next year."

"We know that's the case, Jack," says Steve Quaznik, vice-president of production, that's why we've really got to sell more than a new product. We've got to sell a relationship that the customer can depend on, even if the technology does change."

"What do you mean, 'even if'? We know the technology will change, it's just a matter of whether that will happen just before or just after we launch our campaign for this product."

The group again laughs, but their concerns are serious. With the short lives of high-technology products today, a firm can't afford to make a mistake when launching a new product. The pricing, promotions, and placement of the product has to be right the first time; there won't be a second chance. These elements make up three of the four "P"s, the basics of good marketing in any market. The other "P" stands for Product—what is unique about, and what benefits are gained by the customer when using the product. It is this element that the group is now discussing...

"We know that large motors—specifically large stepping and servo motors—are used extensively in the robotics industry, especially in manufacturing processes," summarizes Dr. Williams. "They are used primarily for simple, repetitive tasks, especially if those tasks involve movements of heavy materials."

"What makes us think there is a market for anything other than simple repetitive tasks in manufacturing environments?" you ask, playing devil's advocate.

"That goes back to our customer surveys, which is where we first identified that there might be a market for the LMCM," Bob contributes. "Labor costs drove large manufacturing concerns, such as those found in the automotive industry. As they sought to be more competitive, they saw they needed to better control their costs, the most significant being labor. When they went to retool to produce smaller cars, they automated a significant portion of their assembly line."

"You still didn't answer my question," you point out.

"Okay, more specifically, when we asked firms if they have current or anticipated needs for greater movement precision for large-horsepower motors, they overwhelmingly responded 'yes.'"

"Where will those needs come from?" you press. "They've already eliminated 80 percent of their labor needs in their new plants."

"They're going for the other 20 percent—those jobs which require greater skill and precision than current automation has been able to provide."

"Unable, that is, until now," Dr. Williams interjects. "I might add that we've just been discussing one industry, and the retooling that is taking place in that industry. This technology, however, has a much broader application in many of the newer industries such as computers, especially in manufacturing of circuit boards, semiconductors, testing, and so on."

The conversation soon turns to a discussion about pricing.

"What will the market bear on this one, Jack?" you ask.

"A better question is to determine what pricing strategy we should have to maximize our profits. I can give you my best guesstimate as to how many LMCMs we will sell at a fixed price, given the current size of the market and our current costs, but that is really just a starting point. We have to consider the longer-term prospects for the product: what is its life-cycle, what is our grace time before we have competition for this product, and what will be the likely response of our current competition to this product."

Jack is finally making a more positive contribution to the discussion for the plans of the new product introduction.

"We want to price the LMCM based upon its value to the customer, not upon our costs to manufacture the product. The faster it can save a buyer money (in saving labor costs, for example) the higher our price should be. Determining value to the customer is not necessarily an easy task, however."

He goes on to explain several possible pricing strategies:

"We can set a relatively low price for the product, much the way Texas Instruments does for its products, to obtain greater unit volume and general acceptance in the market. As our volume increases and our costs decline, we can continue to pass on lower prices to our customers. This pricing strategy will keep other firms from entering the market since they would be less likely to effectively compete with us. Of course, we're not producing the volume that Texas Instruments produces when they make a production run of calculators, for example, but we would still have some impact, especially since we'd be first in the marketplace."

Pricing is an effective deterrent to competition in the marketplace. Although the firm will patent its products, such a step has traditionally offered little protection in the marketplace. A competitor can make a slight change or improvement in the product and claim it is an entirely different product. Likewise, an international competitor— Japan or Korea, for example—can produce the exact same product, knowing that the firm doesn't have the resources, time, or energy to protect its product. Even if the firm does go after an international "copycatter," detente between the firms' governments would most likely prevent any substantial penalties from being incurred. In this regard, a patent serves as little more than a calling card in the market which indicates to a customer that the firm has a committment to producing innovative, "cutting edge" products. In recent years, a new appeals court in Washington, D.C., has made prosecution of patent infringements in the U.S. much easier, but the problem is still far from being resolved in the international marketplace. Jack continues:

"We can set a relatively higher price for the product, much the way Hewlett-Packard does with its new products, and take advantage of our technical innovation and uniqueness in the market. We'll sell fewer units comparatively, but we'll make more per unit. If we are successful, this approach has the disadvantage of attracting other competitors to our market who will produce "copycat" products. In which case we can either keep our prices high and stress the quality of our products, or—as Hewlett-Packard does—lower our prices to still remain competitive and pass on the savings from our 'learning curve.'"

The learning curve is the relationship between direct-hours of labor and the price of a product. As a firm learns how to produce and distribute a product more efficiently, they save money which can be passed on to the customer through a lower price.

Another pricing strategy is to position the product toward the high-quality end of the market, in which case the price is often a secondary issue to the customer. This approach is perhaps more difficult to pursue since it often involves (1) marketing an entire image, not just one product, and (2) more specialized and expensive marketing techniques. It is quite likely that a competitor will sooner or later offer a similar product at a lower price, and undercut your marketing efforts and your position in the market in the process.

A pricing strategy involves planning the method of setting the price over the life of the product, not just at the time of the product's release. What pricing strategy would you like to select for the LMCM?

YOUR CHOICE

1A Low-low: low relative initial price, decreasing as competition increases. See below.

1B Low-high: low relative initial price, increasing as market acceptance occurs. See page 143.

1C High-low: high relative initial price, decreasing as competition increases. See page 143.

1D High-high: high relative price, kept high to reflect quality emphasis. See page 143.

1A **Low-low: low relative initial price, decreasing as lower competition increases.**

This is the safest pricing strategy for both obtaining and maintaining your market share. You are likely to deter potential competitors who would otherwise be interested in entering the market.

+3 Points; Please Go to Decision #2, Page 143.

1B **Low-high: low relative initial price, increasing as market acceptance occurs.**

Your customers are not likely to show much brand loyalty, especially since your firm is small and relatively unknown. When you increase your price, extensive competition is inevitable.

−3 Points; Please Go to Decision #2, below.

1C **High-low: high relative initial price, decreasing as competition increases.**

A good pricing strategy. Your initial acceptance might not be as high as you would like, but you will probably be able to be more competitive in price than any other firm who tries to enter the market later.

+4 Points; Please Go to Decision #2, below.

1D **High-high: high relative price, kept high to reflect quality emphasis.**

You might get away with this for a short while, but you will soon face extensive competition by others who are willing to sell a similar product for less. The "high-quality" angle needs to be a part of your entire company's image, and is less likely to be successful for just one product.

−2 Points; Please Go to Decision #2, below.

Decision #2: New Product Promotions Strategy

Having decided on a pricing strategy for the LMCM, the discussion now turns to promotions for the new product...

"How are we going to get the word out about this product?" you ask.

"The answer to that question entirely depends on another question, namely 'who makes the buying decision,'" Bob interjected. "We have to make sure our promotional efforts are getting through to the decision maker, otherwise they will be in vain."

"You mean, for example, if we were selling children's cereal, we'd want to get our message through to those five-year-olds that will cry in the food store until their mother puts their favorite box into the cart, even though the kids don't themselves have any disposable income?" Barney asks.

"You got it. In the same way, we've got to primarily reach the technical types that make decisions about design approaches and product selections when they are building a manufacturing robot or designing an automated processing line—not purchasing agents, plant managers, or executives of high-tech firms. We have to make sure they are (1) aware of our product, and (2) that they have enough of the necessary information needed to make a purchase decision. With some products, a purchase decision can be made based solely on information read in a sales brochure; other products need more personalized or specific information, such as the tailored applications that could be made to the product. Such specialized information is better handled in a personal manner, such as a sales representative might employ, but we're a small company and can't afford many sales reps at this time."

Finding the prospective buyer, however, is easier said than done. Trade shows, technical journals, advertising, and targeted marketing are all ways to try to let them know about your firm and what you have. Each of these methods has different degrees of effectiveness and costs.

Participating in trade shows is relatively expensive and takes a lot of time and effort to coordinate. You can display a large number of products and meet a wide range of potential buyers, including distributors. Of course, what counts is how many of those contacts translate to sales and in that regard, you're not sure this is the best use of your budget, although there is also something to be said for the general company exposure, which will be increasingly valuable as it grows larger.

Technical journals are without a doubt more effective, especially given the fact that articles are published for free. Of course, that means someone has to write the articles for submission, they have to be well-written and technically accurate to warrant publication, and even then you have no control over which articles will be selected and by which journals.

Alternately, you can purchase advertising in trade magazines. This gets you both product and company exposure, although the coverage is less credible than a trade or journal article. This is also a relatively moderate expense. Overall potential payoffs would be moderate to high.

Targeted marketing, such as sending direct-mail literature to prospective buyers, is another viable alternative. This can also be expensive if you want to have a quality brochure. You're also going to need to buy or create a list of high-prospect names to mail to—a potentially difficult task. Even with a good mailing list, it is uncertain what type of response you can expect other than knowing that most direct-mail literature receives less than a one percent response rate.

What is your first preference for promotions for the LMCM at this time?

YOUR CHOICE

2A Participate in trade shows. See below.

2B Publish articles in trade journals. See page 146.

2C Do targeted marketing. See page 147.

2A **Participate in trade shows.**

This is probably your best bet for initially introducing the product. You'll be able to see who is interested in the product and for what reasons. Trade shows are expensive, but provide a broad exposure for the product.

+3 Points; Please Continue . . .

What is your second preference for promotions at this time?

YOUR CHOICE

(Do not select a choice previously made.)

2B Publish articles in trade journals. See page 146.

2D Do targeted marketing. See page 147.

2E No other promotional activities at this time. See page 148.

2B Publish articles in trade journals.

This means of promotions provides excellent coverage for a high-tech product such as yours, especially for the cost (which is minimal).

+2 Points; Please Continue...

Getting articles published, however, is not necessarily easy. You have to have a timely, well-written article; there still is no guarantee that it will be published; and if it is you have little control over which journal will select it for publication. Even then, since an article would typically be submitted to one journal at a time (by professional etiquette), it can quickly become dated. Probably the biggest challenge is actually producing the articles to begin with. The articles have to be well written and of technical merit and appropriate style.

How do you wish to handle this responsibility?

YOUR CHOICE

2F Hire a professional writer to take on the responsibility of writing journal articles. See page 148.

2G Rotate the responsibility of writing journal articles among your management team. See page 149.

2H Assign the responsibility of writing journal articles to your director of research and development. See page 149.

2I Write the articles yourself as time permits. See page 150.

2C **Do targeted marketing.**

This will probably be a better alternative after you have received a broader exposure for the product.

−1 Point; Please Choose Again:

(Do not select a choice previously made.)

2A Participate in trade shows. See page 145.

2B Publish articles in trade journals. See page 146.

2D **Do targeted marketing.**

This activity should be more successful once you have a better feel for who wants the product and for what purposes.

+2 Points; Please Continue . . .

What type of targeted marketing would you like to do?

YOUR CHOICE

2J Conduct focused advertising. See page 150.

2K Conduct a direct-mail campaign. See page 151.

2L Make selective sales calls. See page 151.

2E No other promotional activities at this time.

You're not going to sell many LMCMs with the limited promotional activities you have selected so far!

−2 Points; Please Choose Again:

(Do not select a choice previously made.)

2A Participate in trade shows. See page 145.

2B Publish articles in trade journals. See page 146.

2D Do targeted marketing. See page 147.

2F Hire a professional writer to take on the responsibility of writing journal articles.

A good choice for making sure that the activity does not become a low priority, as it surely will for practically anyone who does it in-house.

+2 Points; Please Continue…

Are there any other promotional activities you would like to conduct at this time?

YOUR CHOICE

(Do not select a choice previously made.)

2A Participate in trade shows. See page 145.

2C Do targeted marketing. See page 147.

2E No other promotional activities at this time. See page 148.

2G **Rotate the responsibility of writing journal articles among your management team.**

This is going to be neither a popular nor an effective choice! Just exactly how do you expect your vice-president of production to pull off a technical article?? The articles will quite likely fall through the cracks...

−2 Points; Please Continue...

Are there any other promotional activities you would like to select at this time?

YOUR CHOICE

(Do not select a choice previously made.)

2A Participate in trade shows. See page 145.

2C Do targeted marketing. See page 147.

2E No other promotional activities at this time. See page 148.

2H **Assign the responsibility of writing journal articles to your director of research and development.**

He begrudgingly accepts the responsibility, although he makes it clear that this type of activity is why he left academia to come to work for your firm.

−1 Point; Please Continue...

You find out your director of research and development delegated the responsibility to a recent hire in his department. You conclude that the assignment you made wasn't the best decision given the importance of the task. You decide again:

YOUR CHOICE

2F Hire a professional writer to take on the responsibility of writing journal articles. See page 148.

2G Rotate the responsibility of writing journal articles among your management team. See page 149.

2I Write the articles yourself as time permits. See page 150.

2I Write the articles yourself as time permits.

Time won't permit.

−3 Points; Please Continue...

Are there other promotional activities you would like to try?

YOUR CHOICE

(Do not select a choice previously made.)

2A Participate in trade shows. See page 145.

2C Do targeted marketing. See page 147.

2M No other promotional activities at this time. See page 152.

2J Conduct focused advertising.

This is probably your best choice for initial targeted marketing. It narrows your promotions to highly probable prospects, yet is not so focused as to miss potential prospects.

+2 Points; Please Continue...

Do you have any other preferences for promotions at this time?

YOUR CHOICE

2B Publish articles in trade journals. See page 146.

2M No other promotional activities at this time. See page 152.

2K Conduct a direct-mail campaign.

It is not very likely that you will be able to identify and get your material to exactly the right person within the companies which could use your products. This is still, however, worth trying.

+1 Point; Please Continue...

Do you have any other preferences for promotions at this time?

YOUR CHOICE

2B Publish articles in trade journals. See page 146.

2M No other promotional activities at this time. See page 152.

2L Make selective sales calls.

This is not a very efficient means of obtaining additional sales at this time, since you have very few sales representatives.

−2 Points; Please Continue...

Do you have any other preferences for promotions at this time?

YOUR CHOICE

2B Publish articles in trade journals. See page 146.

2M No other promotional activities at this time. See below.

1M No other promotional activities at this time.

Your initial promotional activities seem adequate.

0 Points; Please Go to Decision #3, below.

Decision #3: New Product Distribution Strategy

The group finally turns to discussing placement, or distribution of the new product. For your purposes, this best translates to a decision about how this product will be sold—that is, what channels will be used to distribute the product.

There are a number of factors to be considered in this decision. The more people you put between you and the customer, the more profit you have to give up to someone else. In addition, you lose some market control when you are not the one directly selling and communicating with the customer. If the middleman gives the customer poor service or is unresponsive to the customer's needs or requests, it's you that suffers. Likewise, the customer will not as readily identify the company with the purchased product. This puts your firm at a disadvantage as you are growing and trying to create an overall market awareness that you are a quality producer of an entire line of products.

Possible channels of distribution include: selling the product directly to the customer as an industrial retailer, using either a direct sales force or, (on a more limited basis) assigning regional sales managers to coordinate sales in specific areas.

It is an expensive proposition to hire a sales staff, even if they are primarily paid on a commission basis. There are extensive costs associated with hiring and training such individuals and you will be incurring a large, relatively fixed overhead expense, which will decrease your flexibility—an important consideration during seasonal and/or economic lulls that affect your market. The advantage of having your own sales force, however, is that they are 100 percent dedicated to marketing only your products.

You can also choose to hire manufacturers' representatives, wholesalers, or distributors to sell your product, though it will be difficult to determine exactly how much a manufacturers' representative will represent your interests when he or she is carrying products from a dozen or more companies. And then there is no guarantee that the coverage you do get will be the quality you want or, for that matter, even accurate. A manufacturer's representative can unintentionally or even intentionally misrepresent your product's capabilities to a customer in order to make a sale.

There are financial advantages to using a distributor or wholesaler. They carry an inventory and are responsible for the costs and overhead related to stocking that inventory. They handle a significant administrative burden in invoicing and collecting on accounts, including delinquent accounts. If you use this alternative, you should keep in mind that most distributors expect some type of exclusivity of product distribution and a lengthy contract period. They don't want to be competing with the manufacturer in the market and they don't want to generate a customer base for a product and then have the manufacturer cut them out of the deal.

A compromise of sorts is to hire regional sales managers who serve as dedicated sales representatives and coordinate the overall marketing activities within a specific locale. Such a person might focus on generating new prospective customers, and once a customer is interested, refer them to a distributor which carries the product in their area. This saves administrative time and trouble and allows the sales manager to focus on acquiring new business.

What is your preference for the main method of distributing the LMCM?

YOUR CHOICE

3A Expand your internal sales force. See page 154.

3B Assign regional sales managers. See page 154.

3C Use manufacturers' sales representatives. See page 155.

3D Use distributors and wholesalers. See page 155.

3A **Expand your internal sales force.**

This is an expensive, long-range plan for establishing the product and your firm in the market. You will be able to maintain control over distribution and build a dedicated sales staff, although you will lose some flexibility in your operations.

−2 Points; Please Continue...

Until you are able to fully afford a completely dedicated sales staff, what method of distribution do you prefer?

YOUR CHOICE

3E Assign regional sales managers. See page 156.

3F Use manufacturers' sales representatives. See page 156.

3G Use distributors and wholesalers. See page 156.

3B **Assign regional sales managers.**

This is a good intermediate step that gives you some control, while allowing you to establish a sales organization.

+3 Points; Please Continue...

What is your second preference for a method of distribution?

YOUR CHOICE

3F Use manufacturers' sales representatives. See page 156.

3H Use distributors and wholesalers. See page 156.

3I Expand your internal sales force. See page 157.

3C Use manufacturers' sales representatives.

This is an acceptable temporary approach. You'll have limited control and perhaps some difficulty in finding technically qualified representatives for your product, but you'll remain flexible and avoid locking up financial resources.

+2 Points; Please Continue...

What is your second preference for a method of distribution?

YOUR CHOICE

3E Assign regional sales managers. See page 156.

3H Use distributors and wholesalers. See page 156.

3I Expand your internal sales force. See page 157.

3D Use distributors and wholesalers.

This choice gives you little control over the sales of your product.

−3 Points; Please Continue...

What is your second preference for a method of distribution?

YOUR CHOICE

3E Assign regional sales managers. See page 156.

3F Use manufacturers' sales representatives. See page 156.

3J Expand your internal sales force. See page 157.

3E **Assign regional sales managers.**

An acceptable alternative as the company becomes more established.

+2 Points; Please Go to Decision #4, page 157.

3F **Use manufacturers' sales representatives.**

This alternative provides little control over your product in the marketplace.

−2 Points; Please Go to Decision #4, page 157.

3G **Use distributors and wholesalers.**

This is not a viable option; now that you have your own sales force, you have alienated all distributors and wholesalers.

−4 Points; Please Go to Decision #4, page 157.

3H **Use distributors and wholesalers.**

This is a necessary part of your distribution system for now.

+2 Points; Please Go to Decision #4, page 157.

3I Expand your internal sales force.

This is a good secondary strategy which will help promote future growth and independent control for the company.

+3 Points; Please Go to Decision #4, below.

3J Expand your internal sales force.

Big mistake! All your distributors and wholesalers find out that you are selling directly to their customers and now they refuse to carry any of your products.

−3 Points; Please Go to Decision #4, below.

DECISION #4: BUILD OR BUY

"That's a forlorn look if I've ever seen one!" you joke, walking in on Steve Quaznik, your head of production, as he is deep in deliberation.

"I'm back to the old 'build or buy' dilemma," Steve says. "I sure wish we'd come up with a consistent approach to this issue. Trying to evaluate the quanitative and qualitative issues involved with this problem throws me each time I run into it."

"Maybe it is time we establish a policy on that issue," you say, trying to be encouraging. "What's the problem, anyway?"

The problem is in trying to decide which components of the LMCM should be purchased and which should be built. If you make the wrong choice the firm could lose a substantial amount of money over the next few years and run the risk of being locked into obsolete technology that could seriously dull its competitive edge. Steve had been working out the details of the production and assembly processes for the new LMCM when he became stuck on the build or buy issue.

The LMCM package consists of two units: the motor control mechanism and the motor. The motor control mechanism has several key components, the main one being a control card, a specialized integrated circuit board.

Either of these units could be built in-house less expensively than it would cost to purchase them from another high-tech firm or from a subcontractor specifically hired to do assembly. In fact, most of the subassembly parts (such as circuit boards), could also be made rather than purchased elsewhere. The problem is deciding which to do which way.

Costs are lowest when a component is built by the firm, primarily due to the "learning curve" phenomenon which relates direct-labor hours required to perform a task to the number of times the task has been performed. In other words, the greater the number of components you build, the more efficiently (and inexpensively) you will be able to build them. You also can take advantage of buying supplies in quantity and, of course, you eliminate the profit mark-up that a supplier would have.

Still, building components in-house is not always in the best overall interests of the company. For example, a commitment to completely build a unit in-house will usually require a commitment to certain equipment that is likely to eventually become obsolete (sometimes this occurs sooner than anticipated, as when new technologies are developed). When this happens, the company ends up at a competitive disadvantage with equipment that is underutilized (or no longer used at all).

In addition, building in-house usually requires that additional expertise be brought in, which can increase the overhead and administrative burden on the firm. Increases in capital expenditures and overhead both limit the firm's flexibility in being able to respond quickly to changes in the market.

A big plus in building a product in-house includes a greater control over the quality of the product that is being produced. This is an important factor in the ongoing viability of the company. To some degree, building a product in-house also serves as a way of safeguarding the technology, although it is usually only a matter of time until a competitor has disassembled the product and figured out the basic technology that is employed.

Buying ready-made components allows for greater flexibility of operations and increased liquidity, since financial resources are not tied up in specialized equipment. Buying components can also be a boon in launching your product faster, which will allow you to enter the market sooner—

a big advantage if you believe timing is an important element in the success of the product.

Of course, you can also use a combination of buying and building: buying some components and building others; doing some assembly and having some done by others. IBM uses this split approach, making certain that they always build those parts of their equipment that contain their unique technology. They even go so far as to be sure that sub-components that are built outside of the company are done so by different firms, and if manufactured abroad, by different countries. Then if a country becomes expropriated, for example, they will be unable to make use of the portion of product technology that they have access to.

A final related issue is determining how dependent your firm is upon another firm. You want to be sure that your business does not rely too much on any one other firm for key components to your products. That firm might manipulate the price of the component, or worse, go out of business and leave you stranded. If possible, you should always buy the same components from at least two different suppliers to avoid dependence on any one supplier and to encourage competitive pricing.

There are dozens of firms which produce the type and size motors you need, so that isn't a very scarce or guarded technology. Your problem with motors is that you usually only order a few hundred at a time, thus you don't get much of a price break. Of course, if you had the capability to make motors on demand, it would be a competitive advantage for the company. If you build motors, you could even sell them to others, if that's a market you want to be in.

The motor drives are at the heart of your firm's technology. There are several components in a motor drive, the most important of which is the control card, an integrated circuit board specifically designed for the LMCM. The integrated circuit board is tailored to program the motor drive mechanism. In this regard the component really falls between the motors and the drives both in terms of guarded technology (more than motors, less than motor drives) and availablility of the basic unit from other suppliers (less than motors, more than motor drives).

Given these variables, what is your preferred choice from the following alternatives?

YOUR CHOICE

4A Build motors, drives, and control cards. See below.

4B Buy motors; build drives and control cards. See below.

4C Buy motors and control cards; build drives. See page 161.

4D Buy motors and drives; build control cards. See page 161.

4E Buy motors, drives, and control cards. See page 161.

4A Build motors, drives, and control cards.

This is a poor and unacceptable alternative, since it would require a major shift in your operations, labor, and facilities to start manufacturing all of these items. In addition, building motors, a low-tech product, involves a substantial shift in the focus of your operations. New Age Robotics, is still too small to take on so much.

−5 Points; Please Choose Again:

YOUR CHOICE

4B Buy motors; build drives and control cards. See below.

4C Buy motors and control cards; build drives. See page 161.

4D Buy motors and drives; build control cards. See page 161.

4E Buy motors, drives, and control cards. See page 161.

4B Buy motors; build drives and control cards.

Other firms can make motors and control cards much more efficiently than you could. You should take advantage of their expertise and economies of scale with both items. You were wise to retain the building of the drive unit, especially since it is the key to your new product technology.

+2 Points; Please Go to Decision #5, page 328.

4C **Buy motors and control cards; build drives.**

This is most likely your best alternative. Other firms can build motors and control cards more efficiently than you can, so you should buy those components yet retain control of the drive mechanism, since it contains the unique technology of your new product.

+4 Points; Please Go to Decision #5, page 162.

4D **Buy motors and drives; build control cards.**

Not a good choice. The drive is your unique technology—you should maintain control of it. Motors are low-tech and part of a well-established industry that you would not be able to compete with (in price, resources, quality, and so on) very easily. The control cards can also be made more efficiently by another firm.

−3 Points; Please Go to Decision #5, page 162.

4E **Buy motors, drives, and control cards.**

This will certainly keep your overhead down! You will have maximum flexibility in your operations, but you'll also be entirely dependent upon other firms—a potentially risky position. In addition, you have made it easy for others to obtain your unique technology (the drive unit), which will make it easier for competitors should the market for the LMCM heat up.

−4 Points; Please Go to Decision #5, page 162.

Decision #5: Cutting Costs

Someone left an article on your desk from the *Wall Street Journal* entitled "Cost Cutting Leads to Increased Profits." Circled was a paragraph about midway through the article:

> "In many high-technology companies, cutting costs has never been a priority since sales revenues were always strong. As one executive of a software publishing firm remarked, 'You don't worry about cutting back when the firm is expanding left and right and revenues are doubling every year or two.' As the percentage growth of revenues in such high-tech industries slows, however, or in many cases, declines, attention in those industries is increasingly focused on the expense side of the balance sheet. Indeed, as high-technology industries mature, companies in those industries find that they need to become cost-efficient in order to maintain previous levels of profitability. No industry is immune . . . "

The article is timely in that you have been thinking a lot about costs lately. You are concerned about the company's rising overhead expenses, and what is being done to curtail unnecessary costs on new projects. You bring up the topic of cost-cutting at the next staff meeting. You quote from the article and make the open question: "Are we doing all we can?"

"There always seem to be more ways to cut corners," Jack suggests, "but it's a bit more difficult to gauge when those cuts are going to have a detrimental impact upon quality."

"I agree," Sara states, "we could easily trim our G & A (general and administrative) expenses, for example, but we also might end up leaving more customers on hold on the telephones for longer periods of time or have less technical support when customers have problems with our products and need our assistance."

Dr. Williams chimes in, "Surely research and development could be cut back—even eliminated altogether—but then where would that leave us in a few years hence? I fear short-term cuts will detrimentally effect our long-term priorities."

They all all making valid points, but their arguments don't change the priority of the issue for you. True, any cuts involve trade-offs, and those trade-offs are not always clear. Waste and inefficiency can be tough to pinpoint and more often than not managers feel that other department's funds are excessive— rarely their own. Still, at the same time, you feel a bit on the defensive and attempt to rationalize bringing up the topic at all:

"This isn't an inquisition and I certainly don't want us to abandon the objectives we've so painstakingly developed for our firm. But at the same time, I don't want us to be afraid to reexamine where we stand on important issues such as cost control and what we are doing on a daily basis to keep it an important priority. Take, for example, our recent new product introduction: the LMCM. This product has been in production for over three months now, and I don't believe we've closely examined what costs could be trimmed in its processes. Steve, any thoughts?"

"Well, we'll need to start with identifying what drives the production end of our business. In our case, labor rates are relatively low, since we use semi-skilled labor for a great percentage of our assembly and testing, the main steps of the LMCM production process. Likewise, our resource costs are relatively fixed and competitive. Probably the biggest cost involved with this project was in its initial development, which, by the way, came in at less than was forecasted."

"Perhaps we need to reevaluate our whole research strategy," suggests Sara. "I mean, maybe we should be purchasing new technology from others rather than always trying to develop new technologies in-house."

"I'm certainly not opposed to such an examination," states Dr. Williams. "My department pretty much has its hands full as it is, and of course we'd still need to be closely involved in integrating any new technology with our existing products. Let's not overlook the LMCM, however, and possibilities for savings with that product. We could, for example, increase the line speed of our assembly process; there are several bottlenecks which seem to delay the overall process."

"I'll agree on that point," says Steve. "We run all integrated circuit boards we purchase from suppliers through extensive testing to identify defects. If we were assured of getting top-quality components our testing could be greatly reduced or even completely eliminated."

"We could also initiate a tighter control on expenses by lowering the amount that requires an additional sign-off," Sara suggests. "Right now additional approval is needed only for items over $5000. I'm confident that expenditures would significantly decrease if that amount was lowered to $500. The number of requests always diminish as bureaucratic procedures increase—it's a law of organizational behavior I've noted."

"That's fine and well for your area, Sara, but in my area we don't make those requests unless we need to, and adding approval steps is going to cut into our overall efficiency and how much we're capable of doing," Dr. Williams comments.

"We've been throwing out a lot of ideas," you summarize, "perhaps we should more closely investigate the feasibility of some of them."

What cost-savings idea would you prefer to pursue?

YOUR CHOICE

5A Focus on cutting back general and administrative expenses. See page 165.

5B Focus on purchasing new technologies rather than developing them. See page 165.

5C Focus on bottlenecks in the assembly process of the LMCM. See page 166.

5D Pursue all of these options. See page 166.

5A **Focus on cutting back G & A expenses.**

Although administrative overhead is a popular place for firms to try to cut back, New Age Robotics is actually quite lean. Administrative procedural changes are more likely to be cosmetic with little real savings visible to the firm.

−3 Points, Please Choose Again:

5B Focus on purchasing new technologies rather than developing them. See below.

5C Focus on bottlenecks in the assembly process of the LMCM. See page 166.

5B **Focus on purchasing new technologies rather than developing them.**

This is an interesting possiblity to pursue, unfortunately, you find that purchasing technologies is as expensive as developing new ones in your market.

0 Points; Please Choose Again:

5A Focus on cutting back G & A expenses. See above.

(Choose only if not previously selected.)

5C Focus on bottlenecks in the assembly process of the LMCM. See page 166.

5C Focus on bottlenecks in the assembly process of the LMCM.

This is a good selection to pursue. Costs can often be cut by increasing efficiency of a process.

+2 Points; Please Continue...

In this case, the assembly of the LMCM seems to be bogged down in the testing of integrated circuit boards that go into the motor drives. How would you like to handle this problem?

YOUR CHOICE

5E Require your supplier to test all circuit boards. See page 167.

5F Double the number of circuit boards you test to increase the supply available. See page 167.

5G Buy circuit boards from different suppliers and compare the quality of each based on your testing. See page 167.

5D Pursue all of these options.

I like your style!

+3 Points; Please Continue...

How do you hope to achieve this choice?

YOUR CHOICE

5H Discuss the alternatives and make decisions jointly in your management staff meeting. See page 167.

5I Assign a project to each of your staff members for evaluation and presentation to your staff. See page 168.

5J Assign the topic and suggestions to a committee established for the purpose. See page 168.

5E **Require your supplier to test all circuit boards.**

Your supplier says "No problem!" He then charges you more for the circuit boards you receive to allow for the additional product testing.

−1 Point, Please Go to Decision #6, page 168.

5F **Double the number of circuit boards you test to increase the supply available.**

This gets rid of the bottleneck, but you just increased your cost significantly for additional labor, testing equipment, storage, and so on.

−2 Points; Please Go to Decision #6, page 168.

5G **Buy circuit boards from different suppliers and compare the quality of each based on your testing.**

This is a good idea which should help to increase the competitiveness of both the quality and the price of the circuit boards.

+2 Points, Please Go to Decision #6, page 168.

5H **Discuss the alternatives and make decisions jointly in your management staff meeting.**

It will be difficult to give an adequate amount of time and consideration to each of the alternatives in your staff meetings. Chances are this topic will diminish in importance in your staff meetings as more pressing operating needs emerge.

−1 Points; Please Go to Decision #6, page 168.

5I **Assign a project to each of your staff members for evaluation and presentation to your staff.**

This method of assigning individual responsibility and ownership for cost-cutting ideas in each department will help to keep those ideas a priority for you as well as your staff.

+3 Points; Go to Decision #6, below.

5J **Assign the topic and suggestions to a committee established for the purpose.**

You risk making the topic a lower priority by doing this. Still, it allows another group to make a more thorough investigation of the possibilities and make and evaluate recommendations for you.

+1 Point; Please Go to Decision #6, below.

DECISION #6: A LABOR DISPUTE

"Word has it," Jane Curtain, your administrative assistant, says, "some of the assemblers are dissatisfied."

"Dissatisifed? About what?" you ask, somewhat surprised.

"It seems they feel slighted that they weren't given a chance to bid on new positions created for the LMCM assembly. To them it is just another indication of what little say they have in decisions which affect them; decisions which influence their job security and salaries, for example."

None of the employees at New Age Robotics are unionized, as is typical of most high-technology companies today, and you want to keep it that way so you try to be sensitive to their concerns. You feel a union would greatly reduce the firm's ability to compete and give you less flexibility in operations and decision making. Your assistant continues:

"The way they see it, this firm is profitable and growing fast but little of that gain is being passed on to them. They are excited about working here and glad to be a part of a successful operation, but they want their contributions to the success acknowledged—preferably in their paychecks."

You can't help but be somewhat defensive:

"Don't we already pay competitively? Aren't our benefits better than average? Isn't the working environment here on the posh side? If they want to earn more, they only need to increase their skills or obtain a degree—and aren't we willing to reimburse them for any job-related classes or training that they take?"

Your reaction caught Jane off guard: "Hold on! I'm not complaining; you don't have to convince me that this is a good place to work. I'm just passing on some of the talk I've heard in lunchroom."

Perhaps you are overly sensitive on this topic. In the past unskilled or semi-skilled workers would go to work for a manufacturer, join a union, and depend upon the labor organization to negotiate steady pay increases, and even train them for more highly skilled positions. As union membership has dropped over the years, individuals have had to fend for themselves in the marketplace: obtaining valuable skills and negotiating their own contracts. Often there hasn't been much to negotiate, since available employment in these job categories is usually a "take it or leave it" offer and there are always plenty of people who would take it. But now that many high-tech industries are maturing and their growth is more or less predictable, employee demands have been maturing as well.

You are especially sensitive to the issue because unions represent a threat to the entire robotics industry. Labor usually blames increased automation for part of the hardships they have been facing of late. More workers will be displaced as robotics expands to more industries and replaces more functions within those industries. You sincerely believe that robotics will free workers from the more mundane, boring jobs while at the same time creating new jobs. (A case in point are all the positions at New Age Robotics). This logic, however, is not readily accepted by labor.

You don't want to get caught in a crisis situation on this issue; you don't want to overreact either. After thinking about it you make a decision.

YOUR CHOICE

6A Collect more information about the situation. See below.

6B Take action to correct the problem. See below.

6C Do nothing for now. See page 171.

6A Collect more information about the situation.

It never hurts to gather additional information, especially as there doesn't seem to be a crisis situation requiring immediate action.

+3 Points; Please Continue...

How would you like to go about collecting more information about the situation?

YOUR CHOICE

6D Have your administrative assistant try to get more information about specifically what is being said and by whom. See page 172.

6E Conduct an employee attitude survey to get more information about employee feelings. See page 172.

6F Have your administrative assistant schedule a meeting for you to meet with some of the dissatisfied employees. See page 173.

6B Take action to correct the problem.

Sounds good except you really aren't sure yet what exactly the problem is.

−2 Points; Please Continue...

What corrective action did you have in mind?

YOUR CHOICE

6G Confront the disgruntled employees. See page 174.

6H Initiate a job-posting system that lists open positions for in-house employees. See page 174.

6I Appoint a task force of managers and workers to discuss and make recommendations concerning the issues raised in the attitude survey. See page 175.

6C Do nothing for now.

This is an acceptable alternative for now. You certainly don't want to overreact based upon scant data.

+1 Point; Please Continue . . .

Unfortunately, the situation becomes worse and unionizing talk becomes widespread throughout the company. What do you want to do about it?

YOUR CHOICE

6E Conduct an employee attitude survey to get more information about employee feelings. See page 172.

6F Have your administrative assistant schedule a meeting for you to meet with some of the dissatisfied employees. See page 173.

6I Appoint a task force of managers and workers to discuss and make recommendations concerning the issues raised in the attitude survey. See page 175.

6J Do nothing at this time. See page 175.

6D Have your administrative assistant try to get more information about specifically what is being said and by whom.

This borders on espionage, but who'll be the wiser?

+1 Point; Please Continue...

The additional information she collects is bleak—there are several employees who are advocating unionizing activities. What are you going to do about this?

YOUR CHOICE

6C Do nothing for now. See page 171.

6E Conduct an employee attitude survey to get more information about employee feelings. See below.

6G Confront the disgruntled employees. See page 174.

6E Conduct an employee attitude survey to get more information about employee feelings.

This is a good idea. It gives you a base of information to make decisions from that isn't slanted by just a few dissatisfied employees.

+2 Points; Please Continue...

The attitude survey confirms that there is some employee dissatisfaction, especially concerning the lack of a job-posting system, pay, and job security. What do you want to do with this information?

YOUR CHOICE

6H Initiate a job-posting system that lists open positions for in-house employees. See page 174.

6I Appoint a task force of managers and workers to discuss and make recommendations concerning the issues raised in the attitude survey. See page 175.

6J Do nothing at this time. See page 175.

6K Issue a 5 percent across-the-board raise for nonskilled and semiskilled labor. See page 175.

6F **Have your administrative assistant schedule a meeting for you to meet with some of the dissatisfied employees.**

This is probably not the best decision. It is good that you are showing personal concern; however, you might be setting a precedent for how complaints are handled and thus be giving undue attention and importance to employees who are disgruntled. In addition, you are at a loss for being able to explain how you knew they were dissatisfied...

−2 Points; Please Continue...

The employees make it perfectly clear what their concerns are. They also state they expect changes to be made soon. How do you wish to handle the situation?

YOUR CHOICE

6I Appoint a task force of managers and workers to discuss and make recommendations concerning the issues raised in the attitude survey. See page 175.

6J Do nothing at this time. See page 175.

6L Fire the disgruntled employees. See page 176.

6G Confront the disgruntled employees.

This is a major mistake. Specifically singling out employees is potentially threatening to them and adds credence to their complaints, which could give them undue power in the situation.

−3 Points; Please Continue . . .

The confronted employees file a claim with the National Labor Relations Board and request an investigation of labor practices at New Age Robotics. What would you like to do?

YOUR CHOICE

6C Do nothing for now. See page 171.

6E Conduct an employee attitude survey to get more information about employee feelings. See page 172.

6M Hold a meeting of all employees to discuss the incident. See page 176.

6N Hold a meeting of all managers to discuss the incident. See page 176.

6H Initiate a job-posting system that lists open positions for in-house employees.

This seems a bit hasty, but the immediate problem is resolved and employees seem pleased the company was so responsive.

+2 Points; Please Go to Decision #7, page 177.

6I **Appoint a task force of managers and workers to discuss and make recommendations concerning the issues raised in the attitude survey.**

An excellent choice! It gives you a chance to obtain a greater depth of information on the issues and have some possible solutions developed—any of which you can veto, if necessary.

+3 Points; Please go to Decision #7, page 177.

6J **Do nothing at this time.**

It's not a good policy to seek information from people and then not use it. It makes them feel you were insincere in your initial request.

−2 Points; Please Choose Again:

6H Initiate a job-posting system that lists open positions for in-house employees. See page 174.

6I Appoint a task force of managers and workers to discuss and make recommendations concerning the issues raised in the attitude survey. See above.

6K Issue a 5 percent across-the-board raise for nonskilled and semiskilled labor. See below.

6M Hold a meeting of all employees to discuss the incident. See page 176.

6N Hold a meeting of all managers to discuss the incident. See page 176.

6K **Issue a 5 percent across-the-board raise for nonskilled and semiskilled labor.**

This is a rash and uncalled for reaction which sets a dangerous precedent for dealing with employee dissatisfaction.

−3 Points; Please Go to Decision #7, page 177.

6L **Fire the disgruntled employees.**

An undiplomatic response. A union vote is called for and it passes.

−5 Points; Please Go to Decision #7, page 177.

6M **Hold a meeting of all employees to discuss the incident.**

You are really looking to blow this out of proportion, aren't you? Not an effective approach at this stage.

−3 Points; Please Continue...

One employee asks to be given a chance to speak at the meeting. You oblige. The employee goes into a long prepared speech citing grievances, unfair labor practices, and publically challenges you regarding the employees' right to a union. How would you like to respond to this?

YOUR CHOICE

6L Fire the employee. See above.

6O Thank the employee for his comments and take back control of the meeting. Publically defend yourself and the company's practices. See page 177.

6N **Hold a meeting of all managers to discuss the incident.**

A much better response to this potential threat. In the meeting you discuss a management strategy for responding to this incident, effective communication techniques for dealing with employees, and laws and regulations covering employer activities when faced with a unionizing attempt. Subsequently, your management team is much better prepared to handle a unionizing attempt; in fact, when a vote is called for, it fails decisively.

+3 Points; Go to Decision #7, page 177.

60 **Thank the employee for his comments and take back control of the meeting. Publically defend yourself and the company's practices.**

A diplomatic response. A union vote is called for but fails.

+3 Points; Please Go to Decision #7, below.

Decision #7: Product Liability

You apprehensively opened the Western Union telegram. Telegrams, you've found, mean bad news more often than good news. This one appears to be no exception...

> INDUSTRIAL ACCIDENT AT HOBOKEN CUSTOMER SITE STOP EMPLOYEE HOSPITALIZED—REPORTED GOOD CONDITION STOP LMCM MALFUNCTION INITIALLY BLAMED STOP INVESTIGATION PENDING—DETAILS TO FOLLOW STOP END

Hoboken was one of the customer testing sites for the LMCM prototype that was pending broader market distribution. This accident could seriously set back the LMCM's market introduction or at the very least create some bad press that would likely dampen customer acceptance. You immediately call a staff meeting to discuss the issue and its ramifications. You first give an overview of the situation:

"...so that's all the information we have for now; it seems unclear whether this was a freak accident or one that could have been prevented. In either case, we need to discuss how we are going to respond. On the conservative side, we can recall what few prototypes we have in the market—probably a few hundred or so. At the very least, it seems we should notify those customers who are using the LMCM to caution them about the product."

"Disclosure is always a safe bet, but at the same time I'm a bit apprehensive about alarming customers unnecessarily," says Bob, the new products manager. "Why can't we wait until all the facts are in about what happened, and avoid killing the potential for this product unnecessarily. Who knows? It may turn out to be a human error at the customer site. I surely don't have to remind anyone here of the amount of money and time we've put into this product so far."

"I don't think that money should be the criterion we base this decision on," states Dr. Williams. "Should another incident occur, our good faith in handling the matter would be in question and our exposure greatly increased. I believe we're also taking quite a risk in not immediately notifying customers who are using the LMCM. What's our warranty cover in this situation, anyway?"

Jack answers, "Our expressed warranty covers defects in the product for a one-year period. In practice, however, we are much more liberal: We replace any products which break down regardless of their age and substitute upgraded technology whenever possible—all at no cost to the customer. We've been able to have such a generous replacement policy primarily because we haven't had a significant number of product breakdowns."

New Age Robotics has never been in this position before. Its products don't lend themselves to industrial accidents, since they have few, if any, moving parts and each product is completely encased. The LMCM, however, connects and controls larger motors which power heavy equipment such as mechanical arms. A quick, arbitrary movement of a heavy control arm could jeopardize the safety of individuals who are in close proximity to the machine while it is in operation. It is important for you to act decisively on this matter and, if possible, establish a policy or procedure for dealing with related issues in the future. After weighing your alternatives for action you select from the following:

YOUR CHOICE

7A Recall all LMCMs; issue a press statement. See page 179.

7B Notify all customers currently using LMCMs. See page 179.

7C Wait until details of the cause of the accident are clear before taking any action. See page 180.

7D Fly to Hoboken to personally investigate the incident. See page 180.

7A Recall all LMCMs; issue a press statement.

This is a conservative step which will cost you money in lost existing sales as well as lost future sales. In addition, it seems premature.

−3 Points; Please Continue...

The customer and employee sue your firm. What do you want to do about this?

YOUR CHOICE

7E Discontinue marketing the product until the case is settled. See page 181.

7F Continue marketing the product. See page 181.

7B Notify all customers currently using LMCMs.

This is a safe and relatively cost-free move. It is better that they get the news from you than from a third source.

+2 Points; Please Continue...

The customer and employee sue your firm. What do you want to do about this?

YOUR CHOICE

7E Discontinue marketing the product until the case is settled. See page 181.

7F Continue marketing the product. See page 181.

7G Recall all LMCMs; issue a press statement. See page 181.

7C Wait until details of the cause of the accident are clear before taking any action.

This is probably the best choice. It makes sense to get the facts straight before you take any radical actions.

+3 Points; Please Continue...

The straight facts seem to confirm that the LMCM caused the accident. A heavy control arm made a sudden, abrupt movement which smashed an employee's hand. What would you like to do about this?

YOUR CHOICE

7G Recall all LMCMs; issue a press statement. See page 181.

7H Fly to Hoboken to personally investigate the incident. See page 181.

7D Fly to Hoboken to personally investigate the incident.

This is problably unnecessary, although it does show your concern for the issue.

−1 Point; Please Choose Again:

7A Recall all LMCMs; issue a press statement. See page 179.

7B Notify all customers currently using LMCMs. See page 179.

7C Wait until details of the cause of the accident are clear before taking any action. See page 179.

7E Discontinue marketing the product until the case is settled.

If every company did this, there would be few products on the market. The case could drag on for years after which time your product is likely to be obsolete.

−4 Points; Please Go to Decision #8, page 182.

7F Continue marketing the product.

Smart move! Given the likelihood that you will be able to identify the drive error and place safety features on the product, this is your best choice. Pulling it off the market will be taken as an implicit admission that the product was defective.

+4 Points; Go to Decision #8, page 182.

7G Recall all LMCMs; issue a press statement.

This action seems to be warranted now.

+2 Points; Please Continue...

The customer and employee sue your firm. What do you want to do about this?

YOUR CHOICE

7E Discontinue marketing the product until the case is settled. See above.

7F Continue marketing the product. See above.

7H Fly to Hoboken to personally investigate the incident.

This action shows your concern for the matter. It should help develop goodwill in the situation.

+1 Point; Please Continue...

The customer and employee sue your firm. What do you want to do about this?

YOUR CHOICE

7E Discontinue marketing the product until the case is settled. See page 181.

7F Continue marketing the product. See page 181.

DECISION #8: RAISING CAPITAL

Sara O'Neal, your vice-president of finance is just concluding her presentation to your management team:

"...Our financial priorities at this time, then, are twofold: one, to maintain our cash flow so as to allow for adequate working capital and two, to adequately finance the development of our new products. In respect of this latter point, I recommend that we allocate $1.5 million for the expanded marketing and promotions of the LMCM, a product which has shown great potential since it was released. I'll let Dr. Williams present details of his research with the LMCM. Dr. Williams?"

A strong case is being effectively made to support the latest, most promising product New Age Robotics has under development: the LMCM. The product, a computer-programmable movement-control mechanism designed specifically for high-horsepower motors, has the potential of breaking the company into its largest market yet in the robotics industry. The company has been supporting the development of the LMCM for quite some time and is now at the stage where the product needs a final financial push to be completed.

Dr. Williams, who heads the research and development department at New Age Robotics, presents a status report on the LMCM and a description of the project needs and potential. Everyone present agrees that it is necessary to increase funding on the project; the question is how to best accomplish that. There are several alternatives to choose from, each with its own advantages and disadvantages. The main categories are operations, debt, and stock.

Operations. The firm could support the product development out of operating revenues. This is actually the preferred method of financing research and development, since the degree of risk (and hence, potential loss) is controlled (usually limited to a percentage of sales revenues). This is how the product development has been financed to date.

Unfortunately, this method also puts a limit on the amount of progress that can be made in developing a product. It is difficult to significantly expand efforts on a project, for example, if you don't have the necessary funds for equipment, testing, and personnel needed, especially at the final "prototype" stages of the product's development.

In this case, the budget for the LMCM could be increased if a higher percentage of sales revenues were allocated to the product. Of course, this also means that something else in the budget will lose funds. The funds could come, for example, from forgoing capital expenditures, or cutting back on advertising for a designated period of time.

Debt. The firm could borrow money to invest in the product. The company has little short-term debt and an unused line of credit for $500,000. You could use this line of credit, although its intended purpose is to keep the cash-flow steady, to assure the firm has adequate working capital to meet its operating expenditures throughout the year. Using the line of credit to finance a new product development could jeopardize the safety net the firm currently has.

Alternately, the firm could seek a new bank loan for development of the product, using assets or stock for collateral. It may be that a bank would not lend you additional funds, given the speculative nature of how they will be used, or because of the level of existing debt the company has.

Stock. The firm could raise money by issuing more stock. This could involve another round of venture financing, or even the possibility of having the company "go public" and issue common stock for public trading. Either of these alternatives "dilutes" the current shares of stock which are available, i.e., makes them proportionately worth less. In addition, ownership (and hence control) of the company is relinquished when additional stock is sold. This means that the payoff to existing owners (of which you are one) will be proportionately smaller as the company grows and its equity becomes more valuable. It also means that the direction of the firm could be shifted from its current path, as new owners influence the strategic and operations decisions of the firm. Current management's control of the firm and the firm's future may be greatly diminished—particularly in the case of public ownership.

What is your preference for obtaining additional capital for the development of the LMCM at this time?

YOUR CHOICE

8A Obtain needed capital from operating revenues. See below.

8B Obtain needed capital by increasing debt. See page 185.

8C Obtain needed capital by selling more stock. See page 185.

8A Obtain needed capital from operating revenues.

If you can pull it off, this is your best way to pay for new products development.

+3 Points; Please Continue...

Unfortunately, the current budget is pretty tight. In fact, something has to be cut from the current or future budgets to allow for the funds you need. What is your preference for cutting back?

YOUR CHOICE

8D Cut back on administrative overhead. See page 186.

8E Cut back the advertising budget. See page 186.

8F Forgo planned capital (plant and equipment) expenditures. See page 187.

8G Forgo other planned research and development projects. See page 187.

8B Obtain needed capital by increasing debt.

Not a bad choice, if you can pull it off. Of course you increase the risk that the firm will become overextended, but hey! it's other people's money, right?

+2 Points; Please Continue:

Where would you like to borrow additional funds from?

YOUR CHOICE

8H Use your preapproved business line of credit available at your bank. See page 187.

8I Seek a new business loan for product development from your bank. See page 188.

8J Place a second mortgage on your house. See page 189.

8K Seek a new business loan from another bank. See page 189.

8L Seek needed funds from friends and relatives. See page 190.

8C Obtain needed capital by selling more stock.

This is a tough option to pull off, but you can give it a try. You risk losing more control of the firm.

+1 Point; Please Continue:

What is your preference in issuing more stock?

YOUR CHOICE

8M Seek additional venture capital. See page 190.

8N Sell additional stock the firm owns. See page 191.

8O Seek to take the company public. See page 192.

8D Cut back on administrative overhead.

This is always a safe choice, but not so easy to implement and is unlikely to save you a whole lot of money. New Age Robotics is not that large and is not that wasteful, in other words, there's little fat to be trimmed.

+1 Point; Choose Again:

YOUR CHOICE

8E Cut back the advertising budget. See page 186.

8F Forgo planned capital (plant and equipment) expenditures. See page 187.

8G Forgo other planned research and development projects. See page 187.

8E Cutback the advertising budget.

This is a short-sighted solution! How well do you expect your existing products to do if you undercut your marketing efforts?

−2 Points; Choose Again:

YOUR CHOICE

8B Obtain needed capital by increasing debt. See page 185.

8C Obtain needed capital by selling more stock. See page 185.

8F Forgo other planned capital (plant & equipment) expenditures. See page 187.

8G Forgo other planned research and development projects. See page 187.

8F Forgo planned capital (plant & equipment) expenditures.

This may be a feasible choice, depending upon what cuts were made. Chances are, however, you will be undermining your strategic plan and limit your intended growth.

−1 Point: Choose Again:

YOUR CHOICE

8B Obtain needed capital by increasing debt. See page 185.

8C Obtain needed capital by selling more stock. See page 185.

8G Forgo other planned research and development projects. See below.

8G Forgo other planned research and development projects.

This is clearly robbing Peter to pay Paul! Even if the LMCM is wildly successful, it will have a limited life cycle and other new products will need to be in the works.

−3 Points; Choose Again:

8B Obtain needed capital by increasing debt. See page 185.

8C Obtain needed capital by selling more stock. See page 185.

8H Use your preapproved business line of credit available at your bank.

Well, you've got the money, but if you blow this one your financial padding has just been thinned out. That money was intended to be for cash flow crunches in your operations.

+2 Points; Please Continue . . .

The president of your bank gives you a call the day after you deplete most of your available line of credit. He wants to know if everything is OK. What should you say?

YOUR CHOICE

8P Tell your banker everything is fine. See page 192.

8Q Tell your banker you withdrew needed funds for operating expenses. See page 192.

8R Request an increase in your line of credit from your banker. See page 193.

8I **Seek a new business loan for product development from your bank.**

Your request is denied. Your bank is concerned with your current level of debt and is afraid you are spreading yourself too thin.

−1 Point; Choose Again:

8J Place a second mortgage on your house. See page 189.

8K Seek a new business loan from another bank. See page 189.

8L Seek needed funds from friends and relatives. See page 190.

8J **Place a second mortgage on your house.**

You are serious about this product, aren't you? That's good. Risking your personal assets on a business venture is not too bright, however, especially since your firm is large enough to justify some other means of financing.

−2 Points; Choose Again:

(Do not select any choice you have previously made.)

8H Use your preapproved business line of credit available at your bank. See page 187.

8I Seek a new business loan for product development from your bank. See page 188.

8K **Seek a new business loan from another bank.**

Every bank you go to thinks you are already overextended. They tell you to go to your own bank!

0 Points; Choose Again:

8H Use your preapproved line of credit available at your bank. See page 187.

8I Seek a new business loan for product development from your bank. See page 188.

8J Place a second mortgage on your house. See above.

8L Seek needed funds from friends and relatives.

It is not a good policy to mix your business and personal activities! Although you appear to have high hopes for this product, there are probably not any guarantees you can make about how it will do, thus making it a risky investment. If it bombs, you'll have a lot of folks who are close to you quite upset. Fortunately, no one took you up on your offer anyway...

−3 Points; Choose Again:

8H Use your preapproved business line of credit available at your bank. See page 187.

8I Seek a new business loan for product development from your bank. See page 188.

8J Place a second mortgage on your house. See page 189.

8K Seek a new business loan from another bank. See page 189.

8M Seek additional venture capital.

Your current venture capital financiers, who own 51 percent of the firm, disagree with this strategy.

0 Points; Choose Again:

8N Sell additional stock the firm owns. See page 191.

8O Seek to take the company public. See page 192.

8N **Sell additional stock the firm owns.**

It's not doing much good in the company coffers. You have just reduced the percentage of the firm you own, but you got a significant portion of the money you needed as well.

+2 Points; Please Continue:

You are still short needed funds for the development of the new product. You decide you'll have to borrow the money. Where would you prefer to borrow from?

YOUR CHOICE

8H Use your preapproved business line of credit available at your bank. See page 187.

8I Seek a new business loan for product development from your bank. See page 188.

8J Place a second mortgage on your house. See page 189.

8K Seek a new business loan from another bank. See page 189.

8L Seek needed funds from friends and relatives. See page 190.

8O **Seek to take the company public.**

This will perhaps be a viable option in a few years, but right now your firm is considered to be too new and risky to attract the serious consideration of an underwriter.

−1 Point; Choose Again:

8M Seek additional venture capital. See page 190.

(Choose only if not previously selected.)

8N Sell additional stock the firm owns. See page 191.

8P **Tell your banker everything is fine.**

He says that's good to know and asks specifically about your financials.

0 Points; Choose Again:

8Q Say you withdrew needed funds for operating expenses. See below.

8R Request an increase in your line of credit. See page 193.

8Q **Say you withdrew needed funds for operating expenses.**

He checks into your account more closely and finds out you lied to him. He says that using your preapproved line of credit to finance development of a new product is unacceptable. He places new restrictions on your accounts and expresses deep concern that you have lied to him. Your banking relationship is threatened.

−3 Points; Please Go to Case Analysis, page 194.

8R Request an increase in your line of credit.

Your bank complies! They already have a lot invested with you and they are eager to have you succeed. Giving you more credit is safer from their perspective than funding a new business that is yet unproven.

+ 3 Points; Please Go to Case Analysis, page 194.

New-Product Market Results: Case Analysis

The big payoff is if the LMCM made money for the company, and if so, you are rewarded for your efforts on the project. To find out, tally your total points and look up the corresponding page for results and rationale of how you did.

+40 points or above. See R1, below.

+25 to +39 points. See R2, page 195.

+10 to +24 points. See R3, page 195.

−9 to +9 points. See R4, page 195.

−10 to −24 points. See R5, page 196.

−25 to −39 points. See R6, page 196.

−40 points or below. See R7, page 196.

R1: New Product Grosses $10 Million in First Year (+40 points or above)

You get a promotion and a bonus! You obviously have a lot of business savvy to have scored so high. You have consistently made the best decisions that have helped to successfully launch this new product beyond your most optimistic scenario.

For additional insight into which decisions made an impact, see:

"Decision Analysis," page 192, and then

"Probable Causes for New Product's Success," page 200.

R2: NEW PRODUCT GROSSES $5 MILLION IN FIRST YEAR (+25 to +39 points.)

You get a raise and a bonus! You have made excellent decisions, especially on the matters crucial to the success of this new product.

For additional insight into which decisions made an impact, see:

"Decision Analysis," page 192, and then

"Probable Causes for New Product's Success," page 200.

R3: NEW PRODUCT GROSSES $3 MILLION IN FIRST YEAR (+10 to +24 points.)

You get a bonus! You made a solid return on a new investment, primarily due to your decision-making ability in the situations discussed.

For additional insight into which decisions made an impact, see:

"Decision Analysis," page 192, and then

"Probable Causes for New Product's Success," page 200.

R4: NEW PRODUCT GROSSES BREAKS EVEN IN FIRST YEAR (−9 to +9 points.)

You get a letter of recommendation for your personnel file. You had hoped to do better, but you are pleased with breaking even with this product in its first year. You perhaps made some mediocre decisions or you were inconsistent in your decision making so that the effect of good decisions was negated by ineffective decisions that you made.

For additional insight into which decisions made an impact, see:

"Decision Analysis," page 192, and then...

To see which decisions had positive and negative influence upon the final outcome of this product see both:

"Probable Causes for New Product's Success," page 200 and

"Probable Causes for New Product's Failure," page 202.

R5: New Product Loses $3 Million in First Year (−10 to −24 points.)

You are demoted and transferred to Des Moines. You made a few too many ineffective or poor decisions and the product failed as a result.

For additional insight into which decisions made an impact, see:

"Decision Analysis," page 200, and then

"Probable Causes of New Product's Failure," page 202.

R6: New Product Loses $5 Million in First Year (−25 to −39 points.)

You are fired. Hey! We never said managing was a bed of roses! You made one too many poor decisions, several of which had a direct effect upon the failure of this new product.

For additional insight into which decisions made an impact, see:

"Decision Analysis," page 200, and then

"Probable Causes of New Product's Failure," page 202.

R7: New Product Loses $10 Million in First Year (−40 points or below.)

The company goes bankrupt, you lose your job. You consistently made some poor decisions which allowed this new product to bomb, taking the company with it. Better luck next career!

For additional insight into which decisions made an impact, see:

"Decision Analysis," page 200, and then

"Probable Causes of New Product's Failure," page 202.

DECISION ANALYSIS

Here is a brief summary of what you had to do (and why) to obtain the optimal score for each decision. The first three decisions involved some of the many considerations in the development and introduction of a new product. Specifically, they focused on the importance of the 4 Ps: Product, Price, Promotions, and Place (distribution) in the marketing success of a new product.

DECISION #1: NEW PRODUCT PRICING STRATEGY

Pricing is a difficult issue in business. The best answer in this selection was one which maximized profits—initially by using a high price when you had the advantage of a unique technology, then later lowering the price to discourage and better compete with copy-cat products.

DECISION #2: NEW PRODUCT PROMOTIONS STRATEGY

For a high-technology product in a smaller-sized firm, a successful promotions strategy needs to get the product known (with adequate detail for a selection decision to be made) by the right people (the technical person who would make related purchase decisions). Maximum points were obtained by a strategy which initially obtained broad exposure (tradeshows, trade journals) and then became more focused as the ideal users were identified. Such a selection would allow for maximum cost-effective exposure in the primary market.

DECISION #3: NEW PRODUCT DISTRIBUTION STRATEGY

The conflicting forces in selecting an effective distribution mechanism are exposure, control, flexibility and expense. Those distribution channels which allow for the greatest control over who you are selling to and what you are saying (a direct sales force, regional sales managers) force you to commit resources, thus hampering the flexibility of your assets. Distributors, wholesalers, and manufacturers' sales representatives, on the other hand, allow you to have a great deal of flexibility but less control over the number and quality of sales presentations. An ideal strategy would go from greater flexibility (manufacturers' sales representatives) to greater control (direct sales force) over a period of several years.

DECISION #4: BUILD OR BUY

This is a common and basic decision in most manufacturing environments. A successful approach would have the firm purchasing components from others where it is more economical (in terms of both time and money) to do so. In this case, motors should definitely be purchased, and most likely the drive mechanisms as well. Other companies are better estblished to make these products than you are and making them would require a shift of focus in your operations. Components that contain sensitive or unique technological advances should be more closely controlled and guarded from the competition. Thus, in this case, the control cards should be made in-house.

DECISION #5: CUTTING COSTS

All successful businesses need to have an awareness about cost control and cost cutting. It was difficult to determine in advance which of the choices offered would prove most fruitful in saving the organization money. The highest points were given for trying many possibilities including the analysis of the production process for improvements, comparative shopping for supplies, and delegation of the cost-cutting responsibility to all of your staff.

DECISION #6: A LABOR DISPUTE

You needed to proceed cautiously on this decision. When faced with an ambiguous problem it is best to first seek additional reliable information in a discreet manner. You needed to have an awareness of how quickly a situation such as this one could become explosive and you needed to avoid a polarized stand-off through timely and diplomatic actions. Although you need to be cautious, you lost points if your actions were so late as to be regarded as nonresponsive. Points were also lost if you were too quick to react (with inadequate information) or too accommodating (such behavior can lead to future problems as worker expectations increase).

Decision #7: Product Liability

In a time of ever-increasing insurance premiums and an endless number of lawsuits, managers need to be able to effectively handle a potential liability suit. Again, the emphasis is on deliberate, timely actions and responses that are warranted by the facts and available alternatives.

Decision #8: Raising Capital

Fundamental in any business is the ability to obtain funds for successful operation and expansion as necessary. The highest scores were obtained by careful manipulation of the financing options available to the firm. In one portion, you needed to know what budget items could not be cut without dire consequences to the future of the business. In another portion, you had to have an effective style for working with your bank to obtain additional funds.

Probable Reasons for New Product's Success

The following areas and decision selections had an important influence upon the success of this new product.

Issue / Choice Number	Comments
PRICING	
1C	This pricing strategy (high-low) allowed for maximum initial price skimming in the market, and provided a deterent to new competition.
PROMOTIONS	
2A	This gave you good, broad initial exposure in the market.
2B	This got you to your most likely technical buyers.
DISTRIBUTION	
3C	This gave you broad market exposure with maximum flexibility.
3E	This gave you greater control while maintaining a high degree of flexibility.
OPERATIONS	
4B, 4C	Either of these choices allowed you to take advantage of the expertise and economies of others while maintaining your unique technology.
5C	You were able to cut costs by improving your production efficiency.
8A	You avoided additional debt which helped make you more profitable.

PROBLEM RESOLUTION

6A, 6E, 6I	It was wise to gather more information when you were confronted with an ambiguous problem.
6N	You made a deliberate, planned approach to a potentially explosive situation.
7F	You were decisive during adversity.

Please continue to the Appendix, page 205, for an analysis of your decision-making style and effectiveness.

Probable Reasons for New Product's Failure

If the new product failed, it is likely due to an excessive number of choices from those listed below.

Issue / Choice Number	Comments
PRICING	
1B	This pricing strategy (low-high) didn't allow for high initial profits, and encouraged additional competitors to enter your market.
PROMOTIONS	
2E	Your promotions activity was too limited; exposure and sales suffered.
DISTRIBUTION	
3H	You lost too much control of the product, how it was presented, and to whom in the marketplace.
3I	This selection was too expensive, too soon for the company.
OPERATIONS	
4A	You tried to do too much yourself by building all the components for your product.
4D, 4E	You relenquished your unique technical advantage when you selected either of these choices.
8E, 8G	These cutbacks severely weakened the company.
8J, 8L	These were not very stable sources of funds!

PROBLEM RESOLUTION

6G, 6K, 6L, 6M, 7A, 7E	You acted too soon or without adequate rationale.
7C	You waited too long to act!

Please continue to the Appendix, page 205, for an analysis of your decision-making style and effectiveness.

APPENDIX

You just found out how well you'd hypothetically do in an executive position of three sample industries. By examining the decisions you made in aggregate for these three cases, you can determine the predominant decision-making style that you use, your secondary or fall-back style, and the effectiveness of your decision-making style.

Use the following key to first categorize the decisions you made for each case according to one of three decision-making styles, which vary in the degree of control you exerted. Read the general description of your first and second most frequently selected styles for insight into your decision making behavior.

Many of the decision choices did not vary according to the degree of control and thus are not categorized in this appendix. Each of the decision-making styles was effective at various times. To determine how effective you were in your use of the three decision-making styles you may then examine the Effectiveness Index. The Effectiveness Index will tell you the percentage that your decision style moved you toward your desired objectives, that is, lead to positive results. General remarks about the consistency of your decision making style with the effectiveness of the style follows the Effectiveness Index.

Ranking Your Decision-Making Styles

Case #1

Circle the choices you made during this case:

	Style 1	Style 2	Style 3
Decision 1	1E, 1M, 1Y, 1H, 1R, 1U	1G, 1P, 1Q, 1S	1T, 1X
Decision 2	2B, 2G	2C, 2F, 2H	2A, 2D, 2E, 2I
Decision 3	3F, 3H, 3D	3B, 3C, 3K	3A, 3G, 3I, 3J
Decision 4	4E, 4H, 4J	4B, 4C, 4D, 4I	4A, 4F, 4G
Decision 5	5B	—	5A
Decision 6	6C, 6G	6B, 6F	6A, 6D
Decision 7	—	—	—
Total # circled:	____________	____________	____________

CASE #2

Circle the choices you made during this case:

	Style 1	Style 2	Style 3
Decision 1	1F	1D	1E
Decision 2	—	—	—
Decision 3	3G, 3H, 3K	3B, 3C, 3J	3A, 3D, 3E, 3F, 3I
Decision 4	4D, 4F, 4H, 4I, 4L	4B, 4C	4A, 4E, 4J, 4K
Decision 5	5D, 5E	5A	5B, 5C, 5H
Decision 6	—	6E, 6G, 6H	6A, 6B, 6D, 6F
Decision 7	7A, 7G	7B, 7C, 7F	7D, 7E
Total # circled:	____________	____________	____________

CASE #3

Circle the choices you made during this case:

	Style 1	Style 2	Style 3
Decision 1	—	—	—
Decision 2	2E, 2M	2G	2F, 2H, 2I
Decision 3	—	—	—
Decision 4	—	4B, 4C, 4D	4A, 4E
Decision 5	5J	5A, 5B, 5G	5D, 5E, 5F, 5H, 5I
Decision 6	6C, 6J, 6K 6H, 6I	6D, 6E, 6F, 6L, 6M, 6N, 6O	6A, 6B, 6G,
Decision 7	7C, 7E	7B	7A, 7D, 7F, 7G, 7H
Decision 8	8P	8H, 8I, 8K	8D, 8E, 8F, 8G, 8J, 8K, 8R
Total # circled:	____________	____________	____________

NORMALIZING YOUR SCORE

Now add the total number of circled Decision Selections from each case and multiply the total as indicated below:

	Style 1	Style 2	Style 3
Case #1:			
Case #2:			
Case #3:			
Total # all cases:	__________	__________	__________
	× 2.56	× 2.17	× 1.51
	__________	__________	__________
Normalized score			

Finally, rank your decision making styles according to your normalized score:

> My predominant decision-making style (highest normalized score) is Style #________.
>
> My secondary or back up decision-making style (second highest normalized score) is Style #________.
>
> The decision-making style I use the least (lowest normalized score) is Style #________.

Now go to the next page for a more detailed description of these decision making styles…

Understanding Your Decision-Making Styles

Style 1: Indecisive / Go-Along

The person who uses this decision-making style usually abdicates responsibility regarding the decision being made as well as the resulting consequences. Such decision makers can be indecisive due to a lack of knowledge or information, or they can consciously choose to go along with the desires of others as a path of least resistance, thus requiring the least personal effort and avoiding the most potential conflict. On occasion, this style of decision making is very effective as when an individual follows the desires of his or her superior when that person has strong opinions about something that should be done. Indecisive decision makers will likely be seen as ineffective in an organization since they are less likely to take an active part in managing situations, including responsibilities that are clearly a part of their job.

Style 2: Compromising / Controlled Delay

This style of decision making actively seeks to manage problems by either advocating a new possible action or compromise, or by intentionally waiting and collecting additional data on the situation. In the former case, the compromise usually reflects the needs and constraints of all individuals involved in the situation. In the latter case, the decision maker later acts in a timely manner once adequate information is available. Such a delay is a well thought out strategy for coping with the situation, and is not to be confused with the inaction made by the Style 1 (indecisive/go-along) decision maker, who is more apt to dismiss the situation altogether until a crisis evolves. The Style 2 decision maker is more likely to be effective in organizations in that he or she is able to obtain results and resolutions to problems without an over-reliance upon personal or positional authority. The ability to be flexible with others in the work place and to be able to adjust to constantly changing circumstances and priorities are critical skills to be effective in any organization.

STYLE 3: TAKE-CHARGE / EXTREME ACTION

This decision-making style is characterized by clear, firm decisions defiantly defended. The person makes a stand in defending or advocating a specific position that may not necessarily be a popular or an easy choice to make. This decision maker takes an aggressive role in forcing or advocating an extreme position of action that requires managing conflict, extensive negotiating, peer or superior pressure, etc. This decision-making style will be predominant with those individuals who have a strong bias for action. Such an individual would rather make a decision and be wrong than not make one at all! To be effective, the decision maker must have a knowledge of what priorities and actions will lead to his or her intended objectives, that is, he or she must correctly select when to dig in and when to give in. Such an aggressive decision-making style can wreak havoc on working relationships and eventually alienate the decision maker in his or her work environment if used in excess. When this happens, the individual obtains a reputation for being stubborn, inflexible, and / or incompetent.

YOUR PREDOMINANT DECISION-MAKING STYLE

Your predominant decision-making style is the one you used the most throughout these cases, or in other words, the one that you are most comfortable using. Sometimes the decision-making style that comes most naturally ideally suits the type of environment you work in. For example, many organizations favor individuals who take decisive action and thus an individual with a "take-charge" decision-making style would most likely be successful in such an environment. Most organizations, however, require that an individual be flexible in the decision-making styles that are used and appropriately vary the style to fit the situation. Thus in some situations an individual needs to "take charge" and demand a task be completed as scheduled, or be unwavering in the support of an employee who wants a deviation from a company policy. Other situations would require a give-and-take which could not be achieved with a unilateral decision-making style. Yet in other situations the best decision will be no decision at all: with the individual either ignoring a situation or allowing other events to force a decision or action independent of the individual. One of the primary skills in effective decision-making then, is in knowing (and acting upon the knowledge) when to vary one's approach to a problem so as to achieve the optimal results. You'll gain a sense of your ability to be flexible in an appropriate manner when you calculate your Effectiveness Index on page 212, but first a few words about your secondary decision-making style:

Your Secondary Decision-Making Style

Your secondary decision making style is the one you used the second most throughout these cases, or in other words, the one that tended to serve as a back up style for the situations which you felt your predominant style was not effective. Sometimes the secondary style might be an indicator of the "real you" (or a reflection of your more deeply held beliefs). For example, an individual might typically havc a vcry "compromising" style that he or she uses in most work situations; should an emergency or crisis arise that same individual might revert to a "take-charge" style. In such a case the individual's behavior is saying: "I generally like to be flexible and tolerant in working out situations with others, unless it's something really important—then I want it my way, all others be hanged...."

The real test, however, is the degree of effectiveness in which you employ your decision-making style. To determine how effectively you used the three decision-making styles, turn to the Effectiveness Index on the following page...

EFFECTIVENESS INDEX

To see how effective you were in the use of each decision-making style, reexamine the decision choices you just categorized on pages 206 to 208. On the following pages, circle any of the choices that you had previously selected. These decision choices were more effective and each led to positive points. A few decision selections in these cases might have rationally appeared to be the best selections given the situation, circumstances and amount and type of information that was available to you. Due to factors beyond your control (an unprecedented response, luck, unpredicatble events, etc.), however, these situations still had a negative impact upon your desired objectives. Such decision choices are not listed on the following pages since they did not lead to positive points.

CASE #1: EFFECTIVE DECISION SELECTIONS

Circle the decision selections you made in this case:

	Style 1	Style 2	Style 3
Decision 1	1H, 1R	—	1T, 1X
Decision 2	—	2C, 2F, 2H	2D, 2E(*), 2I
Decision 3	3D	3B, 3C, 3K 3G, 3J	
Decision 4	—	4B, 4C, 4I	4A, 4G
Decision 5	—	—	5A
Decision 6	—	6B, 6F	—
Decision 7	—	—	—
Total # circled:	____________	____________	____________

*Count only if you received positive points for this Decision Selection (that is, if you had previously selected Decision Selection 2F).

Case #2: Effective Choices

Circle the choices you made during this case:

	Style 1	Style 2	Style 3
Decision 1	—	—	1E
Decision 2	—	—	—
Decision 3	3H, 3K	3C, 3J	3D, 3F, 3I
Decision 4	4D	4B, 4C	4G, 4K
Decision 5	5E	5A	5B, 5C, 5H
Decision 6	—	6H	6C, 6D, 6F
Decision 7	7G	7B, 7C, 7H	7D
Total # circled:	________	________	________

Case #3: Effective Decision Selections

Circle the choices you made during this choice:

	Style 1	Style 2	Style 3
Decision 1	—	—	—
Decision 2	—	—	2F
Decision 3	—	—	—
Decision 4	—	4B, 4C	—
Decision 5	5J	5G	5D, 5I
Decision 6	6C	6D, 6E, 6H, 6I	6A, 6N, 6O
Decision 7	7C	7B	7F, 7G, 7H
Decision 8	—	8H	8D, 8R
Total # circled:	________	________	________

Now add the total number of effective Decision Selections from each case (the numbers tallied on the last three pages) and divide that number into the total previous count for each decision-making style as indicated below:

	Style 1	**Style 2**	**Style 3**
Case #1:			
Case #2:			
Case #3:			
Total # effective all cases:	________	________	________
divided into...			
Total # all cases (from page 208):	________	________	________

Now rank your decision-making styles according to their effectiveness:

My most effective decision-making style is Style #________.

My second most effective decision-making style is Style #________.

My least effective decision-making style is Style #________.

Now go to the next page for additional interpretation of these results.

Your Frequency of Effective Decision Making

If your most effective decision-making style is your predominant style... you're in good shape. Either through extreme luck or calculated skill, this relationship indicates that the decision-making style you most employ also gets you the best results. It suggests that you have good judgment in knowing when to use an appropriate decision-making style, with which you are comfortable.

If your most effective decision-making style is your secondary or back up style... this might indicate that you are too hesitant in using a decision-making style that works well for you. Perhaps you are compelled to try another decision-making style first, even though you don't really believe it is best for the situation at hand (others expect you to do things a certain way, you had been trained otherwise, or your organization has certain procedures you need to follow).

If your most effective decision-making style is the one you least commonly use... you either have a good feel for when that one decision style is most appropriate, and you only employ it when necessary, or, possibly, you have a very poor idea of when to vary your decision-making style to fit the situation and your selections randomly associated with effective solutions.

Other useful books from Ten Speed Press

THINKERTOYS
by Michael Michalko

A handbook of business creativity for the 90s. This book shows how anyone can become more creative, and provides dozens of proven techniques for generating innovative new ideas—ideas for new businesses, new products, new sales techniques, markets, and so on. $16.95 paper, 360 pages

THAT'S A GREAT IDEA!
by Tony Husch
and Linda Foust

How to get, evaluate, protect, develop, and sell new product ideas —anything from a silly gizmo to a plan for real estate development. A wealth of possibilities for entrepreneurs, inventors, tinkerers— and anyone who's ever had a great idea. $9.95 paper, 256 pages

THE SMALL BUSINESS TEST
by Colin Ingram

A series of tests, based on detalied analysis of close to 100 small businesses, which allow would-be entrepreneurs to evaluate their strengths and weaknesses and greatly improve their chances of success. $8.95 paper, 96 pages

HOW TO START A BUSINESS WITHOUT QUITTING YOUR JOB
by Philip Holland

Beginning with the assumption that you don't have to quit your "real" job in order to become an entrepreneur, this book proves that it *can* be done. It shows you how to choose the right startup business, how to budget your time, and how to make sure *neither* job suffers. It also discusses financing, liability, how to involve your family and how to decide when (or if) to quit your job. $9.95 paper, 192 pages

THEY SHOOT MANAGERS DON'T THEY?
by Terry Paulson

Any manager can use these people-oriented techniques to improve and maintain morale and create an empowered team of employees. Other chapters cover developing listening skills, using influence properly, and managing *your* manager. $11.95 paper, 192 pages

TEN SPEED PRESS
P.O. Box 7123
Berkeley, California 94707

Available from your local bookstore, or order direct from the publisher. Please include $2.50 shipping & handling for the first book, and 50 cents for each additional book. California residents include local sales tax. Write for your free complete catalog of over 400 books, posters, and tapes.

For VISA or Mastercard orders call (510) 845-8414